D0160580

A BOOK
OF
PRAYERS
for Couples

STORMIE
OMARTIAN

HARVEST HOUSE PUBLISHERS

EUGENE, OREGON

Cover design by Koechel Peterson & Associates, Minneapolis, Minnesota

Cover photo © Jupiterimages / Goodshot / Thinkstock

Back cover author photo © Michael Gomez Photography

A BOOK OF PRAYERS FOR COUPLES
Copyright © 2011 by Stormie Omartian
Published by Harvest House Publishers
Eugene, Oregon 97402
www.harvesthousepublishers.com

ISBN 978-0-7369-4669-8 (padded hardcover)
ISBN 978-0-7369-4670-4 (eBook)

Compilation of:

The Power of a Praying® Wife Book of Prayers
Copyright © 2004 by Stormie Omartian
ISBN 978-0-7369-1985-2

The Power of a Praying® Husband Book of Prayers
Copyright © 2004 by Stormie Omartian
ISBN 978-0-7369-1980-7

The Power of Prayer ™ to Change Your Marriage Book of Prayers
Copyright © 2009 by Stormie Omartian
ISBN 978-0-7369-2054-4

Printed in China

11 12 13 14 15 16 17 18 19 / RDS-SK / 10 9 8 7 6 5 4 3 2 1

The Power of a
PRAYING®
WIFE

BOOK of PRAYERS

STORMIE
OMARTIAN

HARVEST HOUSE PUBLISHERS

EUGENE, OREGON

THE POWER OF A PRAYING® WIFE BOOK OF PRAYERS
Copyright © 2004 by Stormie Omartian
Published by Harvest House Publishers
Eugene, Oregon 97402
www.harvesthousepublishers.com

ISBN 978-0-7369-1985-2

Introduction

When I wrote the book *The Power of a Praying® Wife*, I received countless letters filled with testimonies of restored marriages and changed lives. I was deeply touched by the hearts of women who were willing to do anything to see their marriages become all God wanted them to be. Included in many of the letters were requests to have the prayers in this book made available separately.

In the midst of our busy lives, it's often hard to know how to pray beyond the immediate or urgent. That's why praying from this book will set your mind at peace, knowing that when you have prayed each prayer, you will have covered your husband and your marriage thoroughly. Not only will *he* be blessed, but the rewards will be great for *you*, too. There are blessings that will come to you from God simply because you are praying.

Don't be overwhelmed by the many ways there are to pray for your husband. You don't have to do it all in one day, one week, or even one month. Just pick a prayer, any prayer, and let the Holy Spirit lead you from there. And don't worry about the answers. As long as you look to God as the source of all you want to see happen in your husband and your marriage, you don't have to be concerned about how it will happen. It's *your* job to *pray*. It's *God's* job to *answer*. Leave it in His hands.

— Stormie Omartian —

They cried out to the LORD in their trouble, and He saved them out of their distresses. He sent His word and healed them, and delivered them from their destructions.

Psalm 107:19-20

His Wife

Lord, help me to be a good wife. I fully realize that I don't have what it takes to be one without Your help.

Take my selfishness, impatience, and irritability and turn them into kindness, long-suffering, and the willingness to bear all things.

Take my old emotional habits, mindsets, automatic reactions, rude assumptions, and self-protectiveness, and make me patient, kind, good, faithful, gentle, and self-controlled.

Take the hardness of my heart and break down the walls with Your battering ram of revelation. Give me a new heart and work in me Your love, peace, and joy (Galatians 5:22, 23). I am not able to rise above who I am at this moment. Only You can transform me.

Whatever things you ask when you pray, believe that you receive them, and you will have them. And whenever you stand praying, if you have anything against anyone, forgive him, that your Father in heaven may also forgive you your trespasses.

Mark 11:24-25

Prayer Notes

_____

_____

_____

_____

_____

_____

_____

_____

His Wife

Lord, I confess the times I've been unloving, critical, angry, resentful, disrespectful, or unforgiving toward my husband.

Help me to put aside any hurt, anger, or disappointment I feel and forgive him the way You do—totally and completely, no looking back. Make me a tool of reconciliation, peace, and healing in this marriage. Make me my husband's helpmate, companion, champion, friend, and support.

Help me to create a peaceful, restful, safe place for him to come home to. Teach me how to take care of myself and stay attractive to him. Grow me into a creative and confident woman who is rich in mind, soul, and spirit. Make me the kind of woman he can be proud to say is his wife.

Through wisdom a house is built, and by understanding it is established; by knowledge the rooms are filled with all precious and pleasant riches.

Proverbs 24:3-4

Prayer Notes

His Wife

Lord, I lay all my expectations at Your cross. I release my husband from the burden of fulfilling me in areas where I should be looking to You.

Help me to accept him the way he is and not try to change him. I realize that in some ways he may never change, but at the same time, I release him to change in ways I never thought he could.

I leave any changing that needs to be done in Your hands, fully accepting that neither of us is perfect and never will be.

Only You, Lord, are perfect, and I look to You to perfect us. May we be "perfectly joined together in the same mind and in the same judgment" (1 Corinthians 1:10).

Be kind to one another, tenderhearted, for-giving one another, even as God in Christ forgave you.

Ephesians 4:32

Prayer Notes

_____

_____

_____

_____

_____

_____

_____

_____

_____

_____

_____

His Wife

Lord, teach me how to pray for my husband and make my prayers a true language of love. Where love has died, create new love between us. Show me what unconditional love really is and how to communicate it in a way he can clearly perceive.

Bring unity between us so that we can be in agreement about everything (Amos 3:3). May the God of patience and comfort grant us to be like-minded toward one another, according to Christ Jesus (Romans 15:5).

Make us a team, not pursuing separate, competitive, or independent lives, but working together, overlooking each other's faults and weaknesses for the greater good of the marriage. Help us to pursue the things which make for peace and the things by which one may edify another (Romans 14:19).

Let us not grow weary while doing good, for in due season we shall reap if we do not lose heart.

Galatians 6:9

Prayer Notes

_____

_____

_____

_____

_____

_____

_____

_____

_____

_____

_____

His Wife

Lord, I pray that the commitment my husband and I have to You and to one another will grow stronger and more passionate every day. Enable him to be the head of the home as You made him to be, and show me how to support and respect him as he rises to that place of leadership.

Reveal to me what he wants and needs and show me potential problems before they arise. Breathe Your life into this marriage. Make me a new person, Lord. Give me a fresh perspective, a positive outlook, and a renewed relationship with the man You've given me.

Help me see him with new eyes, new appreciation, new love, new compassion, and new acceptance. Give my husband a new wife, and let it be me.

Ask, and it will be given to you; seek, and you will find; knock, and it will be opened to you. For everyone who asks receives, and he who seeks finds, and to him who knocks it will be opened.

Matthew 7:7-8

Prayer Notes

His Work

*L*ord, I pray that You would bless the work of my husband's hands. May his labor bring not only favor, success, and prosperity, but great fulfillment as well. If the work he is doing is not in line with Your perfect will for his life, reveal it to him. Show him what he should do differently and guide him down the right path.

Give him strength, faith, and a vision for the future so he can rise above any propensity for laziness. May he never run from work out of fear, selfishness, or a desire to avoid responsibility.

On the other hand, help him to see that he doesn't have to work himself to death for man's approval. Give him the ability to enjoy his success without striving for more. Help him to excel, but free him from the pressure to do so.

Do you see a man who excels in his work? He will stand before kings; he will not stand before unknown men.

Proverbs 22:29

Prayer Notes

_____

_____

_____

_____

_____

_____

_____

_____

_____

_____

His Work

God, I pray that You will be Lord over my husband's work. May he bring You into every aspect of it. Give him enough confidence in the gifts You've placed in him to be able to seek, find, and do good work. Open up doors of opportunity for him that no man can close.

Develop his skills so that they grow more valuable with each passing year. Show me what I can do to encourage him. I pray that his work will be established, secure, successful, satisfying, and financially rewarding.

Let him be like a tree planted by the stream of Your living water, which brings forth fruit in due season. May he never wither under pressure, but grow strong and prosper (Psalm 1:3).

*Let the beauty of the L*ORD *our God be upon us, and establish the work of our hands for us; yes, establish the work of our hands.*

Psalm 90:17

Prayer Notes

_____

_____

_____

_____

_____

_____

_____

_____

_____

_____

His Finances

Lord, I commit our finances to You. Be in charge of them and use them for Your purposes.

May my husband and I be good stewards of all that You give us and walk in total agreement as to how it is to be disbursed. I pray that we will learn to live free of burdensome debt.

Where we have not been wise, bring restoration and give us guidance. Show me how I can help increase our finances and not decrease them unwisely. Help us to remember that all we have belongs to You and to be grateful for it.

Do not seek what you should eat or what you should drink, nor have an anxious mind. For all these things the nations of the world seek after, and your Father knows that you need these things. But seek the kingdom of God, and all these things shall be added to you.

Luke 12:29-31

Prayer Notes

His Finances

Lord, I pray that (husband's name) will have wisdom to handle money wisely. Help him make good decisions as to how he spends. Show him how to plan for the future. Teach him to give as You have instructed in Your Word.

I pray that he will find the perfect balance between spending needlessly and being miserly. May he always be paid well for the work he does, and may his money not be stolen, lost, devoured, destroyed, or wasted. Multiply it so that what he makes will go a long way.

I pray that he will not be anxious about finances, but will seek Your kingdom first, knowing that as he does, we will have all we need (Luke 12:31).

My God shall supply all your need according to His riches in glory by Christ Jesus.
                                        Philippians 4:19

Prayer Notes

_____

_____

_____

_____

_____

_____

_____

_____

_____

_____

_____

His Sexuality

Lord, bless my husband's sexuality and make it an area of great fulfillment for him. Restore what needs to be restored, balance what needs to be balanced. Protect us from apathy, disappointment, criticism, busyness, unforgiveness, deadness, or disinterest.

I pray that we make time for one another, communicate our true feelings openly, and remain sensitive to what each other needs. Keep us sexually pure in mind and body, and close the door to anything lustful or illicit that seeks to encroach upon us.

Deliver us from the bondage of past mistakes. Remove completely the effect of any sexual experience—in thought or deed—that has ever happened to us outside of our relationship. Purify us by the power of Your Spirit.

Flee sexual immorality. Every sin that a man does is outside the body, but he who commits sexual immorality sins against his own body. Or do you not know that your body is the temple of the Holy Spirit who is in you, whom you have from God, and you are not your own? For you were bought at a price; therefore glorify God in your body and in your spirit, which are God's.

1 Corinthians 6:18-20

Prayer Notes

_____

_____

_____

_____

_____

_____

_____

His Sexuality

Lord, take away anyone or anything from my husband's life that would inspire temptation to infidelity. Help him to "abstain from sexual immorality" so that he will know "how to possess his own vessel in sanctification and honor" (1 Thessalonians 4:3-4).

I pray that we will desire each other and no one else. Show me how to make myself attractive and desirable to him and be the kind of partner he needs. I pray that neither of us will ever be tempted to think about seeking fulfillment elsewhere. I realize that an important part of my ministry to my husband is sexual. Help me to never use it as a weapon or a means of manipulation by giving and withholding it for selfish reasons.

I commit this area of our lives to You, Lord. May it be continually new and alive. Make it all that You created it to be.

The body is not for sexual immorality but for the Lord, and the Lord for the body.
1 Corinthians 6:13

Prayer Notes

_____

_____

_____

_____

_____

_____

_____

_____

_____

_____

_____

_____

His Affection

Lord, I pray for open physical affection between my husband and me. Enable each of us to lay aside self-consciousness or apathy and be effusive in our display of love.

Help us to demonstrate how much we care for and value each other.

Remind us throughout each day to affectionately touch one another in some way.

Help us to not be cold, undemonstrative, uninterested, or remote. Enable us to be warm, tender, compassionate, loving, and adoring. Break through any hardheadedness on our part that refuses to change and grow. If one of us is less affectionate to the other's detriment, bring us into balance.

Change our habits of indifference so that we can become the husband and wife You called us to be.

So husbands ought to love their own wives as their own bodies; he who loves his wife loves himself. For no one ever hated his own flesh, but nourishes and cherishes it, just as the Lord does the church.

Ephesians 5:28-29

Prayer Notes

His Temptations

Lord, I pray that You would strengthen my husband to resist any temptation that comes his way. Deliver him from evils such as adultery, pornography, drugs, alcohol, gambling, and perversion. Remove temptation especially in the area of (name of specific temptation).

Make him strong where he is weak. Help him to rise above anything that seeks to erect a stronghold in his life. Lord, You've said that "whoever has no rule over his own spirit is like a city broken down, without walls" (Proverbs 25:28).

I pray that (husband's name) will not be broken down by the power of evil, but raised up by the power of God. Help him to take charge over his own spirit and have self-control to resist anything and anyone who becomes a temptation.

No temptation has overtaken you except such as is common to man; but God is faithful, who will not allow you to be tempted beyond what you are able, but with the temptation will also make the way of escape, that you may be able to bear it.

1 Corinthians 10:13

Prayer Notes

_____

_____

_____

_____

_____

_____

_____

_____

His Mind

Lord, I pray for Your protection on my husband's mind. Shield him from the lies of the enemy. Help him to clearly discern between Your voice and any other, and show him how to take every thought captive as You have instructed us to do.

May he thirst for Your Word and hunger for Your truth so that he can recognize wrong thinking. Give him strength to resist lying thoughts. Where the enemy's lies have already invaded his thoughts, cleanse his mind. Lord, You have given me authority "over all the power of the enemy" (Luke 10:19).

By that authority given to me in Jesus Christ, I command any lying spirits away from my husband's mind. I proclaim that You, God, have given (husband's name) a sound mind.

Though we walk in the flesh, we do not war according to the flesh. For the weapons of our warfare are not carnal but mighty in God for pulling down strongholds, casting down arguments and every high thing that exalts itself against the knowledge of God, bringing every thought into captivity to the obedience of Christ.

2 Corinthians 10:3-5

Prayer Notes

_____

_____

_____

_____

_____

_____

_____

His Mind

Lord, I pray that my husband will not entertain confusion in his mind, but will live in clarity. Keep him from being tormented with impure, evil, negative, or sinful thoughts. Enable him to be transformed by the renewing of his mind (Romans 12:2).

Help him to be anxious for nothing, but in everything by prayer and supplication, with thanksgiving, let his requests be made known to You; and may Your peace, which surpasses all understanding, guard his heart and mind through Christ Jesus (Philippians 4:6-7).

And finally, whatever things are true, noble, just, pure, lovely, of good report, having virtue, or anything praiseworthy, let him think on these things (Philippians 4:8).

To be carnally minded is death, but to be spiritually minded is life and peace.

Romans 8:6

Prayer Notes

_____

_____

_____

_____

_____

_____

_____

_____

_____

_____

_____

His Fears

Lord, You've said in Your Word that "there is no fear in love; but perfect love casts out fear, because fear involves torment. But he who fears has not been made perfect in love" (1 John 4:18).

I pray You will perfect my husband in Your love so that tormenting fear finds no place in him. I know You have not given him a spirit of fear. You've given him power, love, and a sound mind (2 Timothy 1:7).

I pray in the name of Jesus that fear will not rule over my husband. Instead, may Your Word penetrate every fiber of his being, convincing him that Your love for him is far greater than anything he faces and nothing can separate him from it.

The angel of the LORD encamps all around those who fear Him, and delivers them.

Psalm 34:7

Prayer Notes

His Fears

Lord, I pray that my husband will acknowledge You as a Father whose love is unfailing, whose strength is without equal, and in whose presence there is nothing to fear. Deliver him this day from fear that destroys and replace it with godly fear (Jeremiah 32:40).

Teach him Your way, O Lord. Help him to walk in Your truth. Unite his heart to fear Your name (Psalm 86:11).

May he have no fear of men, but rise up and boldly say, "The LORD is my helper; I will not fear. What can man do to me?" (Hebrews 13:6). "How great is Your goodness, which You have laid up for those who fear You" (Psalm 31:19).

Fear not, for I am with you; be not dismayed, for I am your God. I will strengthen you, yes, I will help you, I will uphold you with My righteous right hand.

Isaiah 41:10

Prayer Notes

_____

_____

_____

_____

_____

_____

_____

_____

_____

_____

His Fears

I say to you, (husband's name), "Be strong, do not fear! Behold, your God will come with vengeance, with the recompense of God; He will come and save you" (Isaiah 35:4).

"In righteousness you shall be established; you shall be far from oppression, for you shall not fear" (Isaiah 54:14).

"You shall not be afraid of the terror by night, nor of the arrow that flies by day, nor of the pestilence that walks in darkness, nor of the destruction that lays waste at noonday" (Psalm 91:5-6).

May the Spirit of the Lord rest upon you, "the Spirit of wisdom and understanding, the Spirit of counsel and might, the Spirit of knowledge and of the fear of the LORD" (Isaiah 11:2).

I sought the LORD, and He heard me, and delivered me from all my fears.

Psalm 34:4

Prayer Notes

_____

_____

_____

_____

_____

_____

_____

_____

_____

_____

_____

_____

His Purpose

Lord, I pray that (husband's name) will clearly hear the call You have on his life. Help him to realize who he is in Christ and give him certainty he was created for a high purpose. Enable him to walk worthy of his calling and remind him of what You've called him to be. Don't let him get sidetracked with things that are unessential to Your purpose.

Strike down discouragement so that it will not defeat him. Lift his eyes above the circumstances of the moment so he can see the purpose for which You created him. Give him patience to wait for Your perfect timing.

I pray that the desires of his heart will not be in conflict with the desires of Yours. May he seek You for direction and hear when You speak to his soul.

The God of our Lord Jesus Christ, the Father of glory…give to you the spirit of wisdom and revelation in the knowledge of Him, the eyes of your understanding being enlightened; that you may know what is the hope of His calling, what are the riches of the glory of His inheritance in the saints.

Ephesians 1:17-18

Prayer Notes

His Choices

*L*ord, fill my husband with the fear of the Lord and give him wisdom for every decision he makes. May he reverence You and Your ways and seek to know Your truth. Give him discernment to make decisions based on Your revelation. Help him to make godly choices and keep him from doing anything foolish.

I pray that he will listen to godly counselors and not be a man who is unteachable. Instruct him even as he is sleeping (Psalm 16:7), and in the morning, I pray he will do what's right rather than follow the leading of his own flesh. May he not buy into the foolishness of this world, but keep his eyes on You and have ears to hear Your voice.

A wise man will hear and increase learning, and a man of understanding will attain wise counsel.

Proverbs 1:5

Prayer Notes

His Health

Lord, I pray for Your healing touch on (husband's name). Make every part of his body function the way You designed it to.

Wherever there is anything out of balance, set it in perfect working order. Heal him of any disease, illness, injury, infirmity, or weakness.

Strengthen his body to successfully endure his workload, and when he sleeps may he wake up completely rested, rejuvenated, and refreshed.

I pray that he will have the desire to take care of his body, to eat the kind of food that brings health, to get regular exercise, and avoid anything that would be harmful to him. Help him to understand that his body is Your temple and he should care for it as such (1 Corinthians 3:16).

I have heard your prayer, I have seen your tears; surely I will heal you.

2 Kings 20:5

Prayer Notes

_____

_____

_____

_____

_____

_____

_____

_____

_____

_____

_____

His Health

Lord, I pray that You will give my husband a strong heart that doesn't fail. When he is ill, I pray You will sustain him and heal him. Fill him with Your joy to give him strength.

Specifically, I pray for (mention any area of concern). Give him faith to say, "O Lord my God, I cried out to You, and You healed me" (Psalm 30:2). Thank You, Lord, that You are his Healer.

I pray that my husband will live a long and healthy life and when death does come, may it be accompanied by peace and not unbearable suffering and agony.

Thank You, Lord, that You will be there to welcome him into Your presence, and not a moment before Your appointed hour.

They cried out to the LORD in their trouble, and He saved them out of their distresses. He sent His word and healed them, and delivered them from their destructions.

Psalm 107:19-20

Prayer Notes

_____

_____

_____

_____

_____

_____

_____

_____

_____

His Protection

Lord, I pray that You would protect (husband's name) from any accidents, diseases, dangers, or evil influences. Keep him safe, especially in cars and planes. Hide him from violence and the plans of evil people. Wherever he walks, secure his steps. Keep him on Your path so that his feet don't slip (Psalm 17:5).

If his foot does slip, hold him up by Your mercy (Psalm 94:18). Give him the wisdom and discretion that will help him walk safely and not fall into danger (Proverbs 3:21-23).

Save him from any plans of the enemy that seek to destroy his life (Psalm 103:4). Preserve his going out and his coming in from this time forth and even forevermore (Psalm 121:8).

He who dwells in the secret place of the Most High shall abide under the shadow of the Almighty. I will say to the LORD, "He is my refuge and my fortress; my God, in Him I will trust."

Psalm 91:1-2

Prayer Notes

_____

_____

_____

_____

_____

_____

_____

_____

_____

His Trials

Lord, You alone know the depth of the burden my husband carries. I may understand the specifics, but You have measured the weight of it on his shoulders.

I've not come to minimize what You are doing in his life, for I know You work great things in the midst of trials. Nor am I trying to protect him from what he must face.

I only want to support him so that he will get through this battle as the winner. Help him to remember that "the steps of a good man are ordered by the LORD, and He delights in his way. Though he fall, he shall not be utterly cast down; for the LORD upholds him with His hand" (Psalm 37:23-24).

You have been grieved by various trials, that the genuineness of your faith, being much more precious than gold that perishes, though it is tested by fire, may be found to praise, honor, and glory at the revelation of Jesus Christ.

1 Peter 1:6-7

Prayer Notes

His Trials

God, You are our refuge and strength, a very present help in trouble (Psalm 46:1). You have invited us to "come boldly to the throne of grace, that we may obtain mercy and find grace to help in time of need" (Hebrews 4:16).

I come before Your throne and ask for grace for my husband. Strengthen his heart for this battle and give him patience to wait on You (Psalm 27:1-4).

Build him up so that no matter what happens he will be able to stand strong through it. Help him to be always "rejoicing in hope, patient in tribulation, continuing steadfastly in prayer" (Romans 12:12).

Give him endurance to run the race and not give up, for You have said that "a righteous man may fall seven times and rise again" (Proverbs 24:16).

You, who have shown me great and severe troubles, shall revive me again, and bring me up again from the depths of the earth. You shall increase my greatness, and comfort me on every side.

Psalm 71:20-21

Prayer Notes

His Trials

Lord, I pray that in the midst of trials my husband will look to You to be his refuge "until these calamities have passed by" (Psalm 57:1).

May he learn to wait on You because "those who wait on the LORD shall renew their strength; they shall mount up with wings like eagles, they shall run and not be weary, they shall walk and not faint" (Isaiah 40:31).

I pray that he will find his strength in You and as he cries out to You, You will hear him and save him out of all his troubles (Psalm 34:6).

Teach him to cast his burdens on You and let You sustain him through everything that is happening in his life.

As for me, I will call upon God, and the LORD shall save me. Evening and morning and at noon I will pray, and cry aloud, and He shall hear my voice. He has redeemed my soul in peace from the battle that was against me.

Psalm 55:16-18

Prayer Notes

His Integrity

Lord, I pray that You would make my husband a man of integrity, according to Your standards.

Give him strength to say "Yes" when he should say "Yes" and courage to say "No" when he should say "No." Enable him to stand for what he knows is right and not waver under pressure from the world.

Don't let him be a man who is "always learning and never able to come to the knowledge of the truth" (2 Timothy 3:7).

Give him, instead, a teachable spirit that is willing to listen to the voice of wisdom and grow in Your ways.

*The integrity of the upright will guide them,
but the perversity of the unfaithful will destroy
them.*

Proverbs 11:3

Prayer Notes

_____

_____

_____

_____

_____

_____

_____

_____

_____

_____

His Integrity

Lord, I pray that You would make my husband a man who lives by truth. Help him to walk with Your Spirit of truth at all times (John 16:13). Be with him to bear witness to the truth so that in times of pressure he will act on it with confidence (1 John 1:8-9).

Where he has erred in this and other matters, give him a heart that is quick to confess his mistakes. For You have said in Your Word, "If we say that we have no sin, we deceive ourselves, and the truth is not in us" (1 John 1:8).

Don't let him be deceived. Don't let him live a lie in any way. Bind mercy and truth around his neck and write them on the tablet of his heart so he will find favor and high esteem in the sight of God and man (Proverbs 3:3-4).

Better is the poor who walks in his integrity than one perverse in his ways, though he be rich.

Proverbs 28:6

Prayer Notes

_____

_____

_____

_____

_____

_____

_____

_____

_____

_____

_____

His Reputation

Lord, I pray that (husband's name) will have a reputation that is untarnished. I know that a man is often valued "by what others say of him" (Proverbs 27:21), so I pray that he will be respected in our town and people will speak highly of him.

You've said in Your Word that "a curse without cause shall not alight" (Proverbs 26:2).

I pray that there would never be any reason for bad things to be said of him. Keep him out of legal entanglements. Protect us from lawsuits and criminal proceedings. Deliver him from his enemies, O God. Defend him from those who rise up to do him harm (Psalm 59:1).

In You, O Lord, we put our trust. Let us never be put to shame (Psalm 71:1).

*Hide me from the secret plots of the wicked,
from the rebellion of the workers of iniquity,
who sharpen their tongue like a sword, and
bend their bows to shoot their arrows—bitter
words.*

Psalm 64:2-3

Prayer Notes

His Reputation

Lord, Your Word says that "a good tree cannot bear bad fruit, nor can a bad tree bear good fruit. Every tree that does not bear good fruit is cut down and thrown into the fire" (Matthew 7:18-19).

I pray that my husband will bear good fruit out of the goodness that is within him, and that he will be known by the good that he does.

May the fruits of honesty, trustworthiness, and humility sweeten all his dealings so that his reputation will never be spoiled. Preserve his life from the enemy, hide him from the secret counsel of the wicked. Pull him out of any net which has been laid for him (Psalm 31:4).

If You are for us, who can be against us (Romans 8:31)?

Do not let me be ashamed, O LORD, for I have called upon You; let the wicked be ashamed; let them be silent in the grave. Let the lying lips be put to silence, which speak insolent things proudly and contemptuously against the righteous.

Psalm 31:17-18

Prayer Notes

His Reputation

Lord, I pray You would keep my husband safe from the evil of gossiping mouths. Where there has been ill spoken of him, touch the lips of those who speak it with Your refining fire. Let them be ashamed and brought to confusion who seek to destroy his life; let them be driven backward and brought to dishonor who wish him evil (Psalm 40:14).

May he trust in You and not be afraid of what man can do to him (Psalm 56:11). For You have said whoever believes in You will not be put to shame (Romans 10:11).

Lead him, guide him, and be his mighty fortress and hiding place. May his light so shine before men that they see his good works and glorify You, Lord (Matthew 5:16).

Blessed are you when they revile and persecute you, and say all kinds of evil against you falsely for My sake. Rejoice and be exceedingly glad, for great is your reward in heaven, for so they persecuted the prophets who were before you.
Matthew 5:11-12

Prayer Notes

His Priorities

Lord, I pray for my husband's priorities to be in perfect order. Be Lord and Ruler over his heart. Help him to choose a simplicity of life that will allow him to have time alone with You, Lord, a place to be quiet in Your presence every day. Speak to him about making Your Word, prayer, and praise a priority. Enable him to place me and our children in greater prominence in his heart than career, friends, and activities.

I pray he will seek You first and submit his all to You, for when he does I know the other pieces of his life will fit together perfectly.

Help me to properly put my husband before children, work, family, friends, activities, and interests. Show me what I can do right now to demonstrate to him that he has this position in my heart.

Seek first the kingdom of God and His righteousness, and all these things shall be added to you.
                                    Matthew 6:33

Prayer Notes

_____

_____

_____

_____

_____

_____

_____

_____

_____

_____

_____

His Relationships

*L*ord, I pray for (husband's name) to have good, godly male friends with whom he can openly share his heart. May they be trustworthy men of wisdom who will speak truth into his life and not just say what he wants to hear (Proverbs 28:23).

Give him the discernment to separate himself from anyone who will not be a good influence (1 Corinthians 5:13).

Show him the importance of godly friendships and help me encourage him to sustain them.

I pray for strong, peaceful relationships with each of his family members, neighbors, acquaintances, and coworkers. Today I specifically pray for his relationship with (name of person).

Let there be reconciliation and peace where there has been estrangement.

A new commandment I give to you, that you love one another; as I have loved you, that you also love one another. By this all will know that you are My disciples, if you have love for one another.

John 13:34-35

Prayer Notes

_____

_____

_____

_____

_____

_____

_____

_____

_____

His Relationships

Lord, I pray that You would enable my husband to be a forgiving person and not carry grudges or hold things in his heart against others. You've said in Your Word that "he who hates his brother is in darkness and walks in darkness, and does not know where he is going, because the darkness has blinded his eyes" (1 John 2:11).

I pray that my husband would never be blinded by the darkness of unforgiveness, but continually walk in the light of forgiveness. Enable him to love his enemies, bless those who curse him, do good to those who hate him, and pray for those who spitefully use him and persecute him (Matthew 5:44).

I pray that I will be counted as his best friend and our friendship will continue to grow.

If you bring your gift to the altar, and there remember that your brother has something against you, leave your gift there before the altar, and go your way. First be reconciled to your brother, and then come and offer your gift.

Matthew 5:23-24

Prayer Notes

_____

_____

_____

_____

_____

_____

_____

_____

His Fatherhood

Lord, teach (husband's name) to be a good father. Where it was not modeled to him according to Your ways, heal those areas and help him to forgive his dad.

Give him revelation of You and a hunger in his heart to really know You as his heavenly Father. Draw him close to spend time in Your presence so he can become more like You and fully understand Your Father's heart of compassion and love toward him.

Grow that same heart in him for his children. Help him to balance mercy, judgment, and instruction the way You do. Though You require obedience, You are quick to acknowledge a repentant heart. Make him that way, too.

Whom the LORD *loves He corrects, just as a father the son in whom he delights.*

Proverbs 3:12

Prayer Notes

His Fatherhood

Lord, I pray that my husband will understand how to discipline our children properly. May he never provoke his "children to wrath, but bring them up in the training and admonition of the Lord" (Ephesians 6:4).

I pray we will be united in the rules we set for our children and be in full agreement as to how they are raised.

I pray that there will be no strife or argument over how to handle them and the issues that surround their lives. Give him skills of communication with his children.

I pray he will not be thought of by them as stern, hard, cruel, cold, and abusive, but rather may they see him as kind, softhearted, loving, warm, and affirming.

Children's children are the crown of old men,
and the glory of children is their father.
Proverbs 17:6

Prayer Notes

_____
_____
_____
_____
_____
_____
_____
_____
_____
_____
_____

His Fatherhood

Lord, I pray that my husband will inspire his children to honor him as their father so that their lives will be long and blessed. May the spiritual inheritance he passes on to them be one rich in the fullness of Your Holy Spirit. Enable him to model clearly a walk of submission to Your laws.

May he delight in his children and long to grow them up Your way. Help him not to be noncommunicative, passive, critical, weak, uninterested, neglectful, undependable, or uninvolved.

Make him, instead, the kind of father who is interested, affectionate, involved, strong, consistent, dependable, verbally communicative, understanding, and patient. Being a good father is something he wants very much. I pray that You would give him that desire of his heart.

The father of the righteous will greatly rejoice, and he who begets a wise child will delight in him.

Proverbs 23:24

Prayer Notes

His Past

Lord, I pray that You would enable (husband's name) to let go of his past completely. Deliver him from any hold it has on him. Help him to put off his former conduct and habitual ways of thinking about it and be renewed in his mind (Ephesians 4:22-23).

Enlarge his understanding to know that You make all things new (Revelation 21:5).

Show him a fresh, Holy Spirit-inspired way of relating to negative things that have happened. Give him the mind of Christ so that he can clearly discern Your voice from the voices of the past.

When he hears those old voices, enable him to rise up and shut them down with the truth of Your Word.

If anyone is in Christ, he is a new creation; old things have passed away; behold, all things have become new.

2 Corinthians 5:17

Prayer Notes

_____

_____

_____

_____

_____

_____

_____

_____

_____

_____

His Past

Lord, I pray that wherever my husband has experienced rejection in his past, he would not allow that to color what he sees and hears now. Pour forgiveness into his heart so that bitterness, resentment, revenge, and unforgiveness will have no place there. May he regard the past as only a history lesson and not a guide for his daily life.

Wherever his past has become an unpleasant memory, I pray You would redeem it and bring life out of it. Bind up his wounds (Psalm 147:3). Restore his soul (Psalm 23:3).

Help him to release the past so that he will not live in it, but learn from it, break out of it, and move into the future You have for him.

Do not remember the former things, nor consider the things of old. Behold, I will do a new thing, now it shall spring forth; shall you not know it? I will even make a road in the wilderness and rivers in the desert.

Isaiah 43:18-19

Prayer Notes

His Attitude

Lord, fill (husband's name) with Your love and peace today. May there be a calmness, serenity, and sense of well-being established in him because his life is God-controlled, rather than flesh-controlled. Enable him to walk in his house with a clean and perfect heart before You (Psalm 101:2).

Shine the light of Your Spirit upon him and fill him with Your love. I pray that he will be kind and patient, not selfish or easily provoked.

Release him from anger, unrest, anxiety, concerns, inner turmoil, strife, and pressure.

Enable him to bear all things, believe all things, hope all things, and endure all things (1 Corinthians 13:7).

Be anxious for nothing, but in everything by prayer and supplication, with thanksgiving, let your requests be made known to God; and the peace of God, which surpasses all understanding, will guard your hearts and minds through Christ Jesus.

Philippians 4:6-7

Prayer Notes

His Attitude

Lord, I pray that my husband will have a heart of thanksgiving. May he not be broken in spirit because of sorrow (Proverbs 15:13), but enjoy the continual feast of a merry heart (Proverbs 15:15). Give him a spirit of joy and keep him from growing into a grumpy old man.

Help him to be anxious for nothing, but give thanks in all things so he can know the peace that passes all understanding. May he come to the point of saying, "I have learned in whatever state I am, to be content" (Philippians 4:11).

I say to (husband's name) this day, "The LORD bless you and keep you; the LORD make His face shine upon you, and be gracious to you; the LORD lift up His countenance upon you, and give you peace" (Numbers 6:24-26).

Enter into His gates with thanksgiving, and into His courts with praise. Be thankful to Him, and bless His name.

Psalm 100:4

Prayer Notes

_____

_____

_____

_____

_____

_____

_____

_____

_____

His Marriage

Lord, I pray You would protect our marriage from anything that would harm or destroy it. Shield it from our own selfishness and neglect, from the evil plans and desires of others, and from unhealthy or dangerous situations.

May there be no thoughts of divorce or infidelity in our hearts, and none in our future. Set us free from past hurts, memories, and ties from previous relationships, and unrealistic expectations of one another.

I pray that there be no jealousy in either of us, or the low self-esteem that precedes that. Protect us from influences like alcohol, drugs, gambling, pornography, lust, or obsessions. Let nothing come into our hearts and habits that would threaten our marriage in any way.

Two are better than one, because they have a good reward for their labor. For if they fall, one will lift up his companion. But woe to him who is alone when he falls, for he has no one to help him up.

Ecclesiastes 4:9-10

Prayer Notes

_____

_____

_____

_____

_____

_____

_____

_____

_____

_____

His Marriage

Lord, I pray that You would unite my husband and me in a bond of friendship, commitment, generosity, and understanding. Eliminate our immaturity, hostility, or feelings of inadequacy.

Help us to make time for one another alone, to nurture and renew our marriage and remind ourselves of the reasons we were married in the first place.

I pray that (husband's name) will be so committed to You, Lord, that his commitment to me will not waver, no matter what storms come.

I pray that our love for each other will grow stronger every day, so that we will never leave a legacy of divorce to our children.

Now to the married I command, yet not I but the Lord: A wife is not to depart from her husband. But even if she does depart, let her remain unmarried or be reconciled to her husband. And a husband is not to divorce his wife.

1 Corinthians 7:10-11

Prayer Notes

His Emotions

Lord, You have said in Your Word that You redeem our souls when we put our trust in You (Psalm 34:22). I pray that (husband's name) would have faith in You to redeem his soul from negative emotions. May he never be controlled by depression, anger, anxiety, jealousy, hopelessness, fear, or suicidal thoughts.

Specifically I pray about (area of concern). Deliver him from this and all other controlling emotions (Psalm 40:17).

I know that only You can deliver and heal, but use me as Your instrument of restoration. Help me not to be pulled down with him when he struggles. Enable me instead to understand and have words to say that will bring life.

I waited patiently for the LORD; and He inclined to me, and heard my cry. He also brought me up out of a horrible pit, out of the miry clay, and set my feet upon a rock, and established my steps. He has put a new song in my mouth—praise to our God; many will see it and fear, and will trust in the LORD.

Psalm 40:1-3

Prayer Notes

_____

_____

_____

_____

_____

_____

_____

His Emotions

Lord, I pray that You would set my husband free of negative emotions. Release him to share his deepest feelings with me and others who can help.

Liberate him to cry when he needs to and not bottle his emotions inside. At the same time, give him the gift of laughter and ability to find humor in even serious situations.

Teach him to take his eyes off his circumstances and trust in You, regardless of how he is feeling. Give him patience to possess his soul and the ability to take charge of it (Luke 21:9).

Anoint him with "the oil of joy" (Isaiah 61:3), refresh him with Your Spirit, and set him free from any destructive emotions this day.

He who trusts in his own heart is a fool, but whoever walks wisely will be delivered.
Proverbs 28:26

Prayer Notes

His Walk

O Lord, I know the way of man is not in himself; it is not in man who walks to direct his own steps" (Jeremiah 10:23). Therefore, Lord, I pray that *You* would direct my husband's steps. Lead him in *Your* light, teach him *Your* way, so he will walk in *Your* truth.

I pray that he would have a deeper walk with You and an ever-progressing hunger for Your Word. May Your presence be like a delicacy he never ceases to crave.

Lead him on Your path and make him quick to confess when he strays from it. Reveal to him any hidden sin that would hinder him from walking rightly before You. May he experience deep repentance when he doesn't live in obedience to Your laws.

LORD, who may abide in Your tabernacle? Who may dwell in Your holy hill? He who walks uprightly, and works righteousness, and speaks the truth in his heart.

Psalm 15:1-2

Prayer Notes

His Walk

Lord, I pray that You would create a clean heart in my husband and renew a steadfast spirit within him. Don't cast him away from Your presence, and do not take Your Holy Spirit from him (Psalm 51:10-11).

Your Word says that those who are in the flesh cannot please You (Romans 8:8). So I pray that You will enable (husband's name) to walk in the Spirit and not in the flesh and thereby keep himself "from the paths of the destroyer" (Psalm 17:4).

As he walks in the Spirit, may he bear the fruit of the Spirit, which is love, joy, peace, patience, kindness, goodness, faithfulness, gentleness, and self-control (Galatians 5:22-23).

He who walks righteously and speaks uprightly, he who despises the gain of oppressions, who gestures with his hands, refusing bribes, who stops his ears from hearing of bloodshed, and shuts his eyes from seeing evil: he will dwell on high; his place of defense will be the fortress of rocks; bread will be given him, his water will be sure.

Isaiah 33:15-16

Prayer Notes

His Talk

Lord, I pray Your Holy Spirit would guard my husband's mouth so that he will speak only words that edify and bring life. Help him to not be a grumbler, complainer, a user of foul language, or one who destroys with his words, but be disciplined enough to keep his conversation godly.

Your Word says a man who desires a long life must keep his tongue from evil and his lips from speaking deceit (Psalm 34:12-13).

Show him how to do that. Fill him with Your love so that out of the overflow of his heart will come words that build up and not tear down. Work that in my heart as well.

Let no corrupt word proceed out of your mouth, but what is good for necessary edification, that it may impart grace to the hearers.

Ephesians 4:29

Prayer Notes

His Talk

Lord, may Your Spirit of love reign in the words my husband and I speak to each other so that we don't miscommunicate or wound one another. Help us to show each other respect, speak words that encourage, share our feelings openly, and come to mutual agreements without strife.

Lord, You've said in Your Word that when two agree, You are in their midst. I pray that the reverse be true as well—that You will be in our midst so that we two can agree.

Let the words of our mouths and the meditations of our hearts be acceptable in Your sight, O Lord, our strength and our Redeemer (Psalm 19:14).

The words of a wise man's mouth are gracious,
but the lips of a fool shall swallow him up.
Ecclesiastes 10:12

Prayer Notes

_____

_____

_____

_____

_____

_____

_____

_____

_____

_____

_____

His Repentance

Lord, I pray that You would convict my husband of any error in his life. Let there be "nothing covered that will not be revealed, and hidden that will not be known" (Matthew 10:26).

Cleanse him from any secret sins and teach him to be a person who is quick to confess when he is wrong (Psalm 19:12).

Help him to recognize his mistakes. Bring him to full repentance before You. Let his suffering come from a remorseful heart and not because the crushing hand of the enemy has found an opening into his life through unconfessed sin. Lord, I know that humility must come before honor (Proverbs 15:33).

Take away all pride that would cause him to deny his faults and work into his soul a humility of heart so that he will receive the honor You have for him.

Search me, O God, and know my heart; try me, and know my anxieties; and see if there is any wicked way in me, and lead me in the way everlasting.

Psalm 139:23-24

Prayer Notes

_____

_____

_____

_____

_____

_____

_____

_____

_____

_____

$\mathscr{H}$is Deliverance

$\mathscr{L}$ord, You have said to call upon You in the day of trouble and You will deliver us (Psalm 50:15). I call upon You now and ask that You would work deliverance in my husband's life. Deliver him from anything that binds him. Set him free from (name a specific thing). Lift him away from the hands of the enemy (Psalm 31:15).

Bring him to a place of understanding where he can recognize the work of evil and cry out to You for help. If the deliverance he prays for isn't immediate, keep him from discouragement and help him to be confident that You have begun a good work in him and will complete it (Philippians 1:6).

Give him the certainty that even in his most hopeless state, when he finds it impossible to change anything, You, Lord, can change everything.

The LORD is my rock and my fortress and my deliverer; my God, my strength, in whom I will trust; my shield and the horn of my salvation, my stronghold. I will call upon the LORD, who is worthy to be praised; so shall I be saved from my enemies.

Psalm 18:2-3

Prayer Notes

_____

_____

_____

_____

_____

_____

_____

_____

His Deliverance

Lord, help my husband to be strong in You so that he will be delivered from his enemy. Enable him to put on the whole armor of God, so he can stand against the wiles of the devil in the evil day. Help him to gird his waist with truth and put on the breastplate of righteousness, having shod his feet with the preparation of the gospel of peace. Enable him to take up the shield of faith, with which to quench all the fiery darts of the wicked one.

I pray that he will take the helmet of salvation, and the sword of the Spirit, which is the Word of God, praying always with all prayer and supplication in the Spirit, being watchful and standing strong to the end (Ephesians 6:13-18).

Because he has set his love upon Me, therefore I will deliver him; I will set him on high, because he has known My name.

Psalm 91:14

Prayer Notes

His Obedience

Lord, You have said in Your Word that if we regard iniquity in our hearts, You will not hear (Psalm 66:18). I want You to hear my prayers, so I ask You to reveal where there is any disobedience in my life, especially with regard to my husband.

Show me if I'm selfish, unloving, critical, angry, resentful, unforgiving, or bitter toward him. I confess it as sin and ask for Your forgiveness.

I pray that You would also give (husband's name) a desire to live in obedience to Your laws and Your ways. Reveal and uproot anything he willingly gives place to that is not of You. Help him to bring every thought and action under Your control.

Remind him to do good, speak evil of no one, and be peaceable, gentle, and humble (Titus 3:1-2).

My son, do not forget my law, but let your heart keep my commands; for length of days and long life and peace they will add to you. Let not mercy and truth forsake you; bind them around your neck, write them on the tablet of your heart.

Proverbs 3:1-3

Prayer Notes

His Obedience

Lord, I pray that You would give my husband a heart to obey You. Reward him according to his righteousness and according to the cleanness of his hands (Psalm 18:20).

Show him Your ways, O Lord; teach him Your paths. Lead him in Your truth, for You are the God of his salvation (Psalm 25:4-5). Make him a praising person, for I know that when we worship You we gain clear understanding, our lives are transformed, and we receive power to live Your way.

Help him to hear Your specific instructions to him and enable him to obey them. Give him a longing to do Your will and may he enjoy the peace that can only come from living in total obedience to Your commands.

Obey My voice, and I will be your God, and you shall be My people. And walk in all the ways that I have commanded you, that it may be well with you.

Jeremiah 7:23

Prayer Notes

_____

_____

_____

_____

_____

_____

_____

_____

_____

_____

His Self-Image

Lord, I pray that (husband's name) will find his identity in You. Help him to understand his worth through Your eyes and by Your standards. May he recognize the unique qualities You've placed in him and be able to appreciate them.

Enable him to see himself the way You see him, understanding that "You have made him a little lower than the angels, and You have crowned him with glory and honor. You have made him to have dominion over the works of Your hands; You have put all things under his feet" (Psalm 8:4-6).

Quiet the voices that tell him otherwise and give him ears to hear Your voice telling him that it will not be his perfection that gets him through life successfully—it will be Yours.

We all, with unveiled face, beholding as in a mirror the glory of the Lord, are being transformed into the same image from glory to glory, just as by the Spirit of the Lord.

2 Corinthians 3:18

Prayer Notes

His Self-Image

Lord, I pray that You would reveal to my husband that "he is the image and glory of God" (1 Corinthians 11:7), and he is "complete in Him, who is the head of all principality and power" (Colossians 2:10).

Give him the peace and security of knowing that he is accepted, not rejected, by You. Free him from the self-focus and self-consciousness that can imprison his soul.

Help him to see who *You* really are so he'll know who *he* really is. May his true self-image be the image of Christ stamped upon his soul.

I say to you, (husband's name), "Arise, shine; for your light has come! And the glory of the LORD is risen upon you" (Isaiah 60:1).

Whom He foreknew, He also predestined to be conformed to the image of His Son, that He might be the firstborn among many brethren.

Romans 8:29

Prayer Notes

_____

_____

_____

_____

_____

_____

_____

_____

_____

_____

His Faith

Lord, I pray that You will give (husband's name) an added measure of faith today. Enlarge his ability to believe in You, Your Word, Your promises, Your ways, and Your power. Put a longing in his heart to talk with You and hear Your voice.

Give him an understanding of what it means to bask in Your presence and not just ask for things. May he seek You, rely totally upon You, be led by You, put You first, and acknowledge You in everything he does. Lord, You have said in Your Word that "whatever is not from faith is sin" (Romans 14:23).

May my husband be free from the sin of doubt in his life.

Let him ask in faith, with no doubting, for he who doubts is like a wave of the sea driven and tossed by the wind. For let not that man suppose that he will receive anything from the Lord; he is a double-minded man, unstable in all his ways.

James 1:6-8

Prayer Notes

His Faith

Lord, You've said that "faith comes by hearing, and hearing by the word of God" (Romans 10:17). I pray that You would feed my husband's soul with Your Word so his faith grows big enough to believe that with You all things are possible (Matthew 19:26).

Give him unfailing certainty that what You've promised to do, You will do (Romans 4:21). Make his faith a shield of protection. Put it into action to move the mountains in his life. Your Word says, "The just shall live by faith" (Romans 1:17); I pray that he will live the kind of faith-filled life You've called us all to experience.

May he know with complete certainty "how great is Your goodness, which You have laid up for those who fear You, which You have prepared for those who trust in You" (Psalm 31:19).

Having been justified by faith, we have peace with God through our Lord Jesus Christ.

Romans 5:1

Prayer Notes

His Future

Lord, I pray that You would give (husband's name) a vision for his future. Help him to understand that Your plans for him are good and not evil—to give him a future and a hope (Jeremiah 29:11).

Fill him with the knowledge of Your will in all wisdom and spiritual understanding that he may have a walk worthy of You, fully pleasing You, being fruitful in every good work and increasing in the knowledge of You (Colossians 1:9-10).

May he live by the leading of the Holy Spirit and not walk in doubt and fear of what may happen. Help him to mature and grow in You daily, submitting to You all his dreams and desires, knowing that "the things which are impossible with men are possible with God" (Luke 18:27).

I know the thoughts that I think toward you,
says the LORD, thoughts of peace and not of evil,
to give you a future and a hope.

Jeremiah 29:11

Prayer Notes

His Future

Lord, I pray that (husband's name) will always conduct himself in a way that invests in his future. Keep him from losing his sense of purpose and fill him with hope for his future as an "anchor of the soul, both sure and steadfast" (Hebrews 6:19).

Give him "his heart's desire" (Psalm 21:2) and keep him fresh and flourishing and bearing fruit into old age (Psalm 92:13-14).

And when it comes time for him to leave this earth and go to be with You, may he have such a strong vision for his eternal future that it makes his transition smooth, painless, and accompanied by peace and joy. Until that day, I pray he will find the vision for his future in You.

One thing I have desired of the LORD, that will I seek: that I may dwell in the house of the LORD all the days of my life, to behold the beauty of the LORD, and to inquire in His temple.

Psalm 27:4

Prayer Notes

The Power of a
PRAYING®
HUSBAND

BOOK *of* PRAYERS

STORMIE
OMARTIAN

HARVEST HOUSE PUBLISHERS

EUGENE, OREGON

THE POWER OF A PRAYING® HUSBAND BOOK OF PRAYERS

Copyright © 2004 by Stormie Omartian
Published by Harvest House Publishers
Eugene, Oregon 97402
www.harvesthousepublishers.com

ISBN 978-0-7369-1980-7

Covering Your Wife in Prayer

When I wrote *The Power of a Praying® Husband*, I had many requests to have the prayers in that book made into a separate book that could be stuffed in a pocket, slipped into a briefcase, placed in a glove compartment, or propped up on a bedside table or desk. The reason being that most men lead busy lives, and even though they *want* to pray for their wives, they have trouble finding the time. And when they *do* have the time, they struggle with knowing what to pray for and how. If you are one of those men, and I suspect you are or you wouldn't be reading this, these prayers will simplify and enhance your life. Each one of the prayers will probably take less than one minute of your time to pray, but when you have prayed through all the prayers over the coming weeks, you will have covered your wife thoroughly in prayer.

I suggest that you pick a different prayer each day and as you are reminded, pray the prayer one or more times throughout the day. Tell your wife you are going to be praying for her and ask her if there is anything specific she would like you to include in your prayers.

Do not be overwhelmed by how many ways there are to pray for your wife. You don't have to do it all in a day, a week, or even a month. And it's not necessary to pray them in any particular order. Just let the Holy Spirit lead you. Refuse to worry about how and when your prayers will be answered. You don't have to make it happen. It's your job to pray. It's God's job to answer. Leave it in His hands. When you do, you will not only enjoy answers to your prayers, but you will also see great changes in yourself, your wife, and your marriage.

— Stormie Omartian —

The effective, fervent prayer
of a righteous man avails much.

— JAMES 5:16 —

Her Husband

*L*ord, create in *me* a clean heart and renew a right spirit within me (Psalm 51:10). Show me where my attitude and thoughts are not what You would have them to be, especially toward my wife. Convict me when I am being unforgiving. Help me to quickly let go of any anger, so that confusion will not have a place in my mind. If there is behavior in me that needs to change, enable me to make changes that last. Whatever You reveal to me, I will confess to You as sin. Make me a man after Your own heart. Enable me to be the head of my home and family just as You created me to be.

The effective, fervent prayer of
a righteous man avails much.

— JAMES 5:16 —

Prayer Notes

_____

_____

_____

_____

_____

_____

_____

_____

_____

_____

_____

_____

_____

_____

Her Husband

Lord, show me how to really cover (wife's name) in prayer. Enable me to dwell with her with understanding and give honor to her so that my prayers will not be hindered (1 Peter 3:7). Renew our love for one another. Heal any wounds that have caused a rift between us. Give me patience, understanding, and compassion. Help me to be loving, tenderhearted, and courteous to her just as You ask me in Your Word (1 Peter 3:8). Enable me to love her the way that You do.

Husbands ought to love their own wives as their own bodies; he who loves his wife loves himself. For no one ever hated his own flesh, but nourishes and cherishes it, just as the Lord does the church.

— EPHESIANS 5:28-29 —

Prayer Notes

Her Husband

*L*ord, I pray that You would bring (wife's name) and me to a new place of unity with one another. Make us be of the same mind. Show me what I need to do in order to make that come about. Give me words that heal, not wound. Fill my heart with Your love so that what overflows through my speech will be words that build up, not tear down. Convict my heart when I don't live Your way. Help me to be the man, husband, and spiritual leader that You want me to be.

*A man shall leave his father and mother
and be joined to his wife, and the two shall
become one flesh...Let each one of you in
particular so love his own wife as himself, and
let the wife see that she respects her husband.*

— EPHESIANS 5:31,33 —

Prayer Notes

_____

_____

_____

_____

_____

_____

_____

_____

_____

_____

_____

Her Spirit

Lord, I pray that You will give (wife's name) the fulfillment of knowing You in a deeper and richer way than she ever has before. Help her to be diligent and steadfast in her walk with You, never doubting or wavering. Make her strong in spirit and give her an ever-increasing faith that always believes that You will answer her prayers. Help her to carve out time every day to spend with You in Your Word and in prayer and praise. May Your words abide in her, so that when she prays You will give her the desires of her heart.

*If you abide in Me, and My words
abide in you, you will ask what you
desire, and it shall be done for you.*

– JOHN 15:7 –

Prayer Notes

_____

_____

_____

_____

_____

_____

_____

_____

_____

_____

_____

_____

_____

Her Spirit

Lord, as much as I love my wife, I know You love her more. I realize that I cannot meet her every need and expectation, but You can. Help (wife's name) to increase her knowledge of You today. May she turn to You first for everything as You become her constant companion. Give her discernment and revelation and enable her to hear Your voice instructing her. Help her to stay focused on You, no matter how great the storm is around her, so that she never strays off the path You have for her. I pray You would keep me aware of when she needs a fresh filling of Your Spirit so that I will be prompted to pray for her.

*Whoever drinks of the water that I shall give
him will never thirst. But the water that I
shall give him will become in him a fountain
of water springing up into everlasting life.*

– JOHN 4:14 –

Prayer Notes

_____

_____

_____

_____

_____

_____

_____

_____

_____

_____

_____

_____

Her Spirit

*L*ord, help (wife's name) to be so filled with Your Spirit that people sense *Your* presence when they are in *her* presence. As Your daughter, I know she wants to serve You, but help her to understand how and when so that she may glorify You in all she does. Guide her in everything, so that she can become the dynamic, mighty woman of God You want her to be. Give her knowledge of Your will and enable her to stay in the center of it. Help her to trust You will all her heart and not depend on her own understanding. May she acknowledge You in all her ways (Proverbs 3:5-6).

*The Spirit Himself bears witness with
your spirit that we are children of God.*
– ROMANS 8:16 –

Prayer Notes

_____
_____
_____
_____
_____
_____
_____
_____
_____
_____
_____
_____
_____
_____
_____

Her Emotions

*L*ord, I am so grateful that You have made (wife's name) to be a woman of deep thoughts and feelings. I know that You have intended this for good, but I also know that the enemy of her soul will try to use it for evil. Help me to discern when he is doing that and enable me to pray accordingly. Protect her from the author of lies and help her to cast down "every high thing that exalts itself against the knowledge of God, bringing every thought into captivity to the obedience of Christ" (2 Corinthians 10:5).

Keep your heart with all diligence,
for out of it springs the issues of life.
— PROVERBS 4:23 —

Prayer Notes

_____
_____
_____
_____
_____
_____
_____
_____
_____
_____
_____
_____
_____
_____
_____

Her Emotions

*L*ord, give (wife's name) discernment today about what she receives into her mind. I pray she will quickly identify lies about herself, her life, or her future. Help her to recognize when there is a battle going on in her mind and to be aware of the enemy's tactics. Remind her to stick to Your battle plan and rely on the sword of the Spirit, which is Your Word (Ephesians 6:17). Keep me aware of when my wife is struggling so I can talk openly with her about what is on her mind and in her heart. Enable us to communicate clearly so that we don't allow the enemy to enter in with confusion or misinterpretation.

*Do not be conformed to this world, but
be transformed by the renewing of your
mind, that you may prove what is that good
and acceptable and perfect will of God.*

— ROMANS 12:2 —

Prayer Notes

Her Emotions

*L*ord, help me not to react inappropriately or withdraw from (wife's name) emotionally when I don't understand her. Give me patience and sensitivity, and may prayer be my *first* reaction to her emotions and not a last resort. Although I'm aware that I cannot meet my wife's every emotional need, I know that *You* can. I am not trying to absolve myself from meeting any of her needs, but I know that some of them are intended to be met only by You. I pray that You would fill her with Your peace and joy today.

The LORD redeems the soul of His servants, and none of those who trust in Him shall be condemned.

— PSALM 34:22 —

Prayer Notes

_____

_____

_____

_____

_____

_____

_____

_____

_____

_____

_____

_____

_____

_____

Her Emotions

*L*ord, I pray that when certain negative emotions threaten her happiness, You will be the first one (wife's name) runs to, because only You can deliver her from them. Help her to hide herself in "the secret place of Your presence" (Psalm 31:20). I pray that You would restore her soul (Psalm 23:3), heal her brokenheartedness, and bind up her wounds (Psalm 147:3). Make her to be secure in Your love and mine. Take away all fear, doubt, and discouragement, and give her clarity, joy, and peace. Help her to be quick to call on Your mighty name.

The name of the LORD is a strong tower;
the righteous run to it and are safe.

— PROVERBS 18:10 —

Prayer Notes

_____

_____

_____

_____

_____

_____

_____

_____

_____

_____

_____

_____

_____

_____

_____

Her Motherhood

*L*ord, I pray You will help (wife's name) to be the best mother to our children (child) that she can be. Give her strength, and help her to understand that she can do all things through Christ who strengthens her (Philippians 4:13). Give her patience, kindness, gentleness, and discernment. Guard her tongue so that the words she speaks will build up and not tear down, will bring life and not destruction. Guide her as she makes decisions regarding each child. I also bring before You my own concerns about (name any area of concern that you have for that child). I trust that You will help us be the best parents we can be.

Her children rise up and call her blessed;
her husband also, and he praises her.

— PROVERBS 31:28 —

Prayer Notes

_____
_____
_____
_____
_____
_____
_____
_____
_____
_____
_____
_____
_____
_____
_____
_____

Her Motherhood

*L*ord, I know that (wife's name) and I cannot successfully raise our children without You. So I ask that You would take the burden of raising them from our shoulders and partner with us to bring them up. Give (wife's name) and me patience, strength, and wisdom to train, teach, discipline, and care for each child. Help us to understand each child's needs and know how to meet them. Give us discernment about what we allow into the home through TV, books, movies, video games, magazines, and computer activities. Give us revelation and the ability each day to see what we need to see.

Pour out your heart like water before the
face of the LORD. Lift your hands toward
Him for the life of your young children.

— LAMENTATIONS 2:19 —

Prayer Notes

_____

_____

_____

_____

_____

_____

_____

_____

_____

_____

_____

_____

_____

Her Motherhood

*L*ord, show (wife's name) and me Your perspective on each of our children's uniqueness and potential for greatness. Give us a balance between being overprotective and allowing our children to experience life too early. I ask You for the gifts of intelligence, strength, talent, wisdom, and godliness to be in our children. Keep them safe from any accident, disease, or evil influence. May no plan of the enemy succeed in their lives. Help (wife's name) and me to raise our children (child) to be obedient and respectful to both of us and to have a heart to follow You and Your Word. I pray that my wife will find fulfillment, contentment, and joy as a mother, while never losing sight of who she is in You.

They shall not labor in vain, nor bring forth children for trouble; for they shall be the descendants of the blessed of the LORD, and their offspring with them.

— Isaiah 65:23 —

Prayer Notes

_____

_____

_____

_____

_____

_____

_____

_____

_____

_____

_____

_____

Her Moods

Lord, I pray for (wife's name) and ask that You would calm her spirit, soothe her soul, and give her peace today. Drown out the voice of the enemy, who seeks to entrap her with lies. Help her to take every thought captive so she is not led astray (2 Corinthians 10:5). Where there is error in her thinking, I pray You would reveal it to her and set her back on course. Help her to hear Your voice only. Fill her afresh with Your Holy Spirit and wash away anything in her that is not of You.

I will hear what God the LORD will speak, for He will speak peace to His people and to His saints...
— PSALM 85:8 —

Prayer Notes

_____

_____

_____

_____

_____

_____

_____

_____

_____

_____

_____

_____

_____

_____

Her Moods

Lord, I pray that You would balance my wife's body perfectly today so that she is not emotionally carried up and down like a roller coaster. Give (wife's name) inner tranquility that prevails no matter what is going on around her. Enable her to see things from Your perspective so that she can fully appreciate all the good that is in her life. Keep her from being blinded by fear and doubt. Show her the bigger picture, and teach her to distinguish the valuable from the unimportant.

*You will keep him in perfect peace, whose
mind is stayed on You, because he trusts in You.*
– Isaiah 26:3 –

Prayer Notes

_____

_____

_____

_____

_____

_____

_____

_____

_____

_____

_____

_____

_____

_____

Her Moods

Lord, help (wife's name) to recognize the answers to her own prayers. Show me how to convince her that I love her, and help me to be able to demonstrate it in ways she can perceive. I know that You have "called us to peace" (1 Corinthians 7:15). Help us both to hear that call and live in the peace that passes all understanding. I say to my wife, "Let the peace of God rule" in your heart, and "be thankful" (Colossians 3:15).

*The peace of God, which surpasses all
understanding, will guard your hearts
and minds through Christ Jesus.*

– PHILIPPIANS 4:7 –

Prayer Notes

Her Marriage

Lord, I pray that You would establish in me and (wife's name) bonds of love that cannot be broken. Show me how to love my wife in an ever-deepening way that she can clearly recognize. May we have mutual respect and admiration for each other so that we become and remain one another's greatest friend, champion, and unwavering support. Where love has been diminished, lost, destroyed, or buried under hurt and disappointment, put it back in our hearts. Give us strength to hold on to the good in our marriage, even in those times when one of us doesn't *feel* love.

*This is My commandment, that you
love one another as I have loved you.*

— JOHN 15:12 —

Prayer Notes

_____

_____

_____

_____

_____

_____

_____

_____

_____

_____

_____

_____

_____

_____

_____

Her Marriage

*L*ord, enable (wife's name) and me to forgive each other quickly and completely. Specifically I lift up to You (name any area where forgiveness is needed). Help us to "be kind to one another, tenderhearted, forgiving," the way You are to us (Ephesians 4:32). Give us a sense of humor, especially as we deal with the hard issues of life. Unite us in faith, beliefs, standards of morality, and mutual trust. Help us to be of the same mind, to move together in harmony, and to quickly come to mutual agreements about our finances, our children, how we spend our time, and any other decisions that need to be made.

Therefore, as the elect of God, holy and beloved, put on tender mercies, kindness, humility, meekness, longsuffering; bearing with one another, and forgiving one another...
– COLOSSIANS 3:12-13 –

Prayer Notes

_____

_____

_____

_____

_____

_____

_____

_____

_____

_____

_____

_____

_____

Her Marriage

Lord, where (wife's name) and I are in disagreement and this has caused strife, I pray You would draw us together on the issues. Adjust our perspectives to align with Yours. Make our communication open and honest so that we avoid misunderstandings. May we have the grace to be tolerant of each other's faults and, at the same time, have the willingness to change. I pray that we will not live two separate lives, but will instead walk together as a team. Remind us to take time for one another so that our marriage will be a source of happiness, peace, and joy for us both.

*Behold, how good and how pleasant it
is for brethren to dwell together in unity!*

— PSALM 133:1 —

Prayer Notes

_____

_____

_____

_____

_____

_____

_____

_____

_____

_____

_____

_____

_____

_____

Her Marriage

Lord, I pray that You would protect our marriage from anything that would destroy it. Take out of our lives anyone who would come between us or tempt us. Help (wife's name) and me to immediately recognize and resist temptation when it presents itself. I pray that no other relationship either of us have, or have had in the past, will rob us of anything in our relationship now. Sever all unholy ties in both of our lives. May there never be any adultery or divorce in our future to destroy what You, Lord, have put together.

*But the Lord is faithful, who will
establish you and guard you from the evil one.*
— 2 Thessalonians 3:3 —

Prayer Notes

_____

_____

_____

_____

_____

_____

_____

_____

_____

_____

_____

_____

_____

_____

Her Submission

Lord, I submit myself to You this day. Lead me as I lead my family. Help me to make all decisions based on Your revelation and guidance. As I submit my leadership to You, enable (wife's name) to fully trust that You are leading me. Help her to understand the kind of submission You want from her. Help me to understand the kind of submission You want from me. Enable me to be the leader You want me to be. I pray that I will allow You, Lord, to be so in control of my life that my wife will be able to freely trust Your Holy Spirit working in me.

*Wives, submit to your own husbands,
as to the Lord. For the husband is head
of the wife, as also Christ is head of the
church; and He is the Savior of the body.*

— EPHESIANS 5:22-23 —

Prayer Notes

_____

_____

_____

_____

_____

_____

_____

_____

_____

_____

_____

_____

Her Submission

Lord, where (wife's name) and I disagree on certain issues, help us to settle them in proper order. Help me to love my wife the way You love me, so that I will gain her complete respect and love. Give her a submissive heart and the faith she needs to trust me to be the spiritual leader in our home. At the same time, help both of us to submit "to one another in the fear of God" (Ephesians 5:21). I know that only You, Lord, can make that perfect balance happen in our lives.

Husbands, love your wives, just as Christ also loved the church and gave Himself for her...

— EPHESIANS 5:25 —

Prayer Notes

_____

_____

_____

_____

_____

_____

_____

_____

_____

_____

_____

_____

_____

_____

Her Relationships

$\mathcal{L}$ord, I pray for (wife's name) to have good, strong, healthy relationships with godly women. May each of these women add strength to her life and be a strong prayer support for her. I also pray for good relationships with all family members. May Your spirit of love and acceptance reign in each one. I pray for a resolution of any uncomfortable in-law relationships for either of us. Show me what I can do or say to make a positive difference. Specifically I pray for my wife's relationship with (name of friend or family member). Bring reconciliation and restoration where that relationship has broken down.

The righteous should choose his friends carefully,
for the way of the wicked leads them astray.
— PROVERBS 12:26 —

Prayer Notes

_____

_____

_____

_____

_____

_____

_____

_____

_____

_____

_____

_____

_____

_____

Her Relationships

Lord, I pray that (wife's name) will be a forgiving person. Show her that forgiveness doesn't make the other person right, it makes *her free*. If she has any unforgiveness she is unaware of, reveal it to her so she can confess it before You and be released from it. I especially pray that there would be no unforgiveness between us. Enable us to forgive one another quickly and completely. Remind us often that You, Lord, are the only One who knows the whole story, so we don't have the right to judge. Make my wife a light to her family, friends, co-workers, and community, and may all her relationships be glorifying to You, Lord.

Whenever you stand praying, if you have anything
against anyone, forgive him, that your Father
in heaven may also forgive you your trespasses.
— MARK 11:25 —

Prayer Notes

_____

_____

_____

_____

_____

_____

_____

_____

_____

_____

_____

_____

_____

Her Priorities

$\mathcal{L}$ord, show (wife's name) how to seek You first in all things, and to make time with You her first priority every day. Give her the wisdom to know how to effectively divide up her time, and then to make the best use of it. Show her the way to prioritize her responsibilities and interests and still fulfill each role she has to the fullest. Show her how to find a good balance between being a wife, taking care of children and others, running a home, doing her work, serving in the church and community, and finding time for herself so that she can be rested and refreshed.

*To everything there is a season, a
time for every purpose under heaven.*

— ECCLESIASTES 3:1 —

Prayer Notes

_____

_____

_____

_____

_____

_____

_____

_____

_____

_____

_____

_____

_____

Her Priorities

*L*ord, release (wife's name) from the guilt that can weigh her down when things get out of balance. In the midst of all that she does, I pray that she will take time for me without feeling she is neglecting other things. Give her the energy and the ability to accomplish all she needs to do, and may she have joy in the process. Give (wife's name) the grace to handle the challenges she faces each day, and the wisdom to not try to do more than she can. Teach her to clearly recognize what her priorities should be, and enable her to balance them well.

*Seek first the kingdom of God
and His righteousness, and all
these things shall be added to you.*

– MATTHEW 6:33 –

Prayer Notes

_____

_____

_____

_____

_____

_____

_____

_____

_____

_____

_____

_____

Her Priorities

Lord, help (wife's name) to make our home a peaceful sanctuary. Regardless of our financial state, give her the wisdom, energy, strength, vision, and clarity of mind to transform our dwelling into a beautiful place of refuge that brings joy to each of us. Show me how I can encourage and assist her in that. Holy Spirit, I invite You to fill our home with Your peace, truth, love, and unity. Through wisdom let our house be built, and by understanding may it be established. Reveal to us anything that is in our house that is not glorifying to You, Lord. I say that "as for me and my house, we will serve the LORD" (Joshua 24:15).

She watches over the ways of her household,
and does not eat the bread of idleness.

— PROVERBS 31:27 —

Prayer Notes

_____

_____

_____

_____

_____

_____

_____

_____

_____

_____

_____

_____

_____

_____

_____

_____

Her Beauty

Lord, I pray that You would give (wife's name) the "incorruptible beauty of a gentle and quiet spirit, which is very precious" in Your sight (1 Peter 3:4). Help her to appreciate the beauty You have put in her. Make my wife beautiful in every way, and may everyone else see the beauty of Your image reflected in her, but remind her that time spent in Your presence is the best beauty treatment of all. Help me to remember to encourage her and speak words that will make her feel beautiful.

One thing I have desired of the LORD, that will I seek: that I may dwell in the house of the LORD all the days of my life, to behold the beauty of the LORD, and to inquire in His temple.

– PSALM 27:4 –

Prayer Notes

_____

_____

_____

_____

_____

_____

_____

_____

_____

_____

_____

_____

Her Beauty

$\mathcal{L}$ord, where anyone in the past has convinced (wife's name) that she is unattractive and less than who You made her to be, I pray that You would replace those lies with Your truth. I pray that she will not base her worth on appearance, but on Your Word. Convince her of how valuable she is to You, so that I will be better able to convince her of how valuable she is to me. Show my wife how to take good care of herself. Give her wisdom about the way she dresses and adorns herself so that it always enhances her beauty to the fullest and glorifies You.

The King will greatly desire your beauty;
because He is your Lord, worship Him.

— PSALM 45:11 —

Prayer Notes

_____

_____

_____

_____

_____

_____

_____

_____

_____

_____

_____

_____

_____

_____

Her Sexuality

*L*ord, I pray that You would bless (wife's name) today, and especially bless our marriage and our sexual relationship. Help me to be unselfish and understanding toward her. Help her to be unselfish and understanding toward me. Teach us to show affection to one another in ways that keep romance and desire alive between us. Where one of us is more affectionate than the other, balance that out. Help us to remember to touch each other in an affectionate way every day. I pray that how often we come together sexually will be agreeable to both of us.

Let each man have his own wife, and let each woman have her own husband. Let the husband render to his wife the affection due her, and likewise also the wife to her husband.

— 1 Corinthians 7:2-3 —

Prayer Notes

_____

_____

_____

_____

_____

_____

_____

_____

_____

_____

_____

_____

Her Sexuality

Lord, show me if I ever hurt (wife's name), and help me to apologize in a way that will cause her to forgive me completely. Any time we have an argument or a breakdown of communication, enable us to get over it quickly and come back together physically so no room is made for the devil to work. If ever the fire between us dies into a suffocating smoke, I pray that You would clear the air and rekindle the flame.

*Marriage is honorable among
all, and the bed undefiled.*

— Hebrews 13:4 —

Prayer Notes

_____
_____
_____
_____
_____
_____
_____
_____
_____
_____
_____
_____
_____
_____

Her Sexuality

$\mathcal{L}$ord, help me to always treat (wife's name) with respect and honor and never say anything that would demean her, even in jest. Help me to be considerate of her when she is exhausted or not feeling well. But I also pray that she would understand my sexual needs and be considerate of those as well. Only You can help us find that balance. Make our sexual relationship fulfilling, enjoyable, freeing, and refreshing for both of us. May our intimacy bond the two of us together and connect our hearts and emotions as well as our bodies. Help us to freely communicate our needs and desires to one another.

The wife does not have authority over her own body, but the husband does. And likewise the husband does not have authority over his own body, but the wife does.

— 1 CORINTHIANS 7:4 —

Prayer Notes

_____

_____

_____

_____

_____

_____

_____

_____

_____

_____

_____

_____

_____

Her Sexuality

Lord, keep my wife's heart and my heart always faithful. Take out of our lives anyone or anything that would cause temptation. Where there has been unfaithfulness in thought or deed on the part of either of us, I pray for full repentance, cleansing, and release from it. Keep us free from anything that would cause us to neglect this vital area of our lives. May our desire always be only for each other. Renew and revitalize our sexual relationship, and make it all You created it to be.

Therefore what God has joined
together, let no man separate.
– MARK 10:9 –

Prayer Notes

_____

_____

_____

_____

_____

_____

_____

_____

_____

_____

_____

_____

_____

_____

_____

Her Fears

Lord, I pray that You would help (wife's name) to "be anxious for nothing" (Philippians 4:6).

Remind her to bring all her concerns to You in prayer so that Your peace that passes all understanding will permanently reside in her heart. Specifically I pray about (anything that causes your wife to have fear). I ask You to set her free from that fear and comfort her this day. I stand against any enemy attacks targeted at my wife, and I say that a spirit of fear will have no place in her life. Strengthen her faith in You, Lord, to be her Defender.

I sought the LORD, and He heard me,
and delivered me from all my fears.

— PSALM 34:4 —

Prayer Notes

_____

_____

_____

_____

_____

_____

_____

_____

_____

_____

_____

_____

_____

_____

Her Fears

Lord, enable (wife's name) to rise above the criticism of others and be delivered from fear of their opinions. May her only concern be with pleasing you. I say to my wife, "Be strong in the Lord and in the power of His might" (Ephesians 6:10). "In righteousness you shall be established; you shall be far from oppression, for you shall not fear; and from terror, for it shall not come near you" (Isaiah 54:14). Enable my wife to rise up and say, "The LORD is my light and my salvation; whom shall I fear? The LORD is the strength of my life; of whom shall I be afraid?" (Psalm 27:1).

*The fear of man brings a snare, but
whoever trusts in the LORD shall be safe.*

– PROVERBS 29:25 –

Prayer Notes

_____

_____

_____

_____

_____

_____

_____

_____

_____

_____

_____

_____

_____

Her Fears

$\mathcal{L}$ord, give (wife's name) strength in the tough times of her life. Sustain her with Your presence so that nothing will shake her. Enable her to rise above the things that challenge her. Specifically I lift up to You (your wife's greatest need, weakness, struggle, or temptation). Help her separate herself from that which tempts her. I say to (wife's name) that "no temptation has overtaken you except such as is common to man; but God is faithful, who will not allow you to be tempted beyond what you are able, but with the temptation will also make the way of escape, that you may be able to bear it" (1 Corinthians 10:13).

God has not given us a spirit of fear, but
of power and of love and of a sound mind.

– 2 TIMOTHY 1:7 –

Prayer Notes

_____

_____

_____

_____

_____

_____

_____

_____

_____

_____

_____

_____

_____

Her Fears

*L*ord, give (wife's name) patience while she is waiting for her prayers to be answered and for all things to be accomplished. Help her to wait upon You instead of waiting for things to change. Cause her to fear only You and to be content where she is this moment, knowing that You will not leave her there forever. Perfect her in Your "perfect love" that "casts out fear," so that fear has no room in her soul (1 John 4:18). Remind her to "wait on the LORD; be of good courage, and He shall strengthen your heart" (Psalm 27:14).

*I wait for the LORD, my soul
waits, and in His word I do hope.*

— PSALM 130:5 —

Prayer Notes

_____

_____

_____

_____

_____

_____

_____

_____

_____

_____

_____

_____

_____

Her Purpose

$\mathcal{L}$ord, I know that You have placed within (wife's name) special gifts and talents that are to be used for Your purpose and Your glory. Show her what they are, and show me too, Lord, that I may encourage her. Help her to know that You have something in particular for her to do and have given her a ministry that only she can fulfill. Give her a sense of Your call on her life, and open doors of opportunity for her to develop and use her gifts in that calling. Bring her into alignment with Your ultimate purpose for her life, and may she be fulfilled in it.

*In Him also we have obtained an inheritance,
being predestined according to the purpose of
Him who works all things according to the
counsel of His will, that we who first trusted
in Christ should be to the praise of His glory.*

— EPHESIANS 1:11-12 —

Prayer Notes

_____

_____

_____

_____

_____

_____

_____

_____

_____

_____

_____

Her Purpose

Lord, I pray that (wife's name) will be the wife You have called her to be and the wife I need her to be. What I need most from my wife right now is (name the need most pressing on your heart). Show me what my wife needs from me. Help us to fulfill one another in these areas without requiring of each other more than we can be. Keep us from having unrealistic expectations of each other when our expectations should be in You. Help us to recognize the gifts You have placed in each of us and to encourage one another in their development and nurture.

Having then gifts differing according to the grace that is given to us, let us use them...

— ROMANS 12:6 —

Prayer Notes

_____

_____

_____

_____

_____

_____

_____

_____

_____

_____

_____

_____

Her Purpose

Thank You, Lord, for the wife You have given me (Proverbs 19:14). Release her into Your perfect plan for her life so that she will fulfill the destiny You've given her. Use her gifts and talents to bless others. I say to (wife's name), you are "like a fruitful vine in the very heart of your house" (Psalm 128:3). "Many daughters have done well, but you excel them all" (Proverbs 31:29). "Let your light so shine before men, that they may see your good works and glorify your Father in heaven" (Matthew 5:16). Lord, grant my wife according to her heart's desire, and fulfill all her purpose (Psalm 20:4).

[It is God] who has saved us and called us with a holy calling, not according to our works, but according to His own purpose and grace which was given to us in Christ Jesus before time began.

– 2 TIMOTHY 1:9 –

Prayer Notes

Her Trust

Lord, I pray that You would give (wife's name) the ability to trust me in all things. Most of all, I want her to trust Your Holy Spirit working in me and through me. Where I have not been worthy of that trust, show me, and I will confess that before You as sin. Help me not to conduct myself that way anymore. Make me always be worthy of her trust. Show me how to convince her that I am in partnership with You and will do all I can to be trustworthy. Increase our faith, for I know that You are a shield to those who put their trust in You (Proverbs 30:5).

As for God, His way is perfect; the
word of the LORD is proven; He is
a shield to all who trust in Him.

— 2 SAMUEL 22:31 —

Prayer Notes

_____

_____

_____

_____

_____

_____

_____

_____

_____

_____

_____

_____

Her Trust

Lord, where (wife's name) has lost trust in me unjustly, I pray You would help her to see the truth. If she doesn't trust me because of something someone else has done to her, help her to forgive that person so she can be free. I pray that she will not project those failures onto me and expect that I will do the same thing. Specifically I pray about (name any area where there is a lack of trust). Wherever we have broken trust with one another, help us to reestablish it and make it strong. May we both trust You, Lord, working in each of us.

Let him trust in the name of the
LORD and rely upon his God.

— ISAIAH 50:10 —

Prayer Notes

Her Trust

Lord, break any unholy bonds or soul ties between me and any other woman in my past. Break any unholy bonds or soul ties between my wife and any other man in her past. Help us to fully repent of all relationships outside of our own that were not glorifying to You. Lord, I pray that You would deepen my trust of my wife. Show me if there are places where I don't trust her judgment, her abilities, her loyalty, or her decisions. I pray that she will always be a trustworthy person and that I will be able to trust her completely.

*Cause me to hear Your lovingkindness in
the morning, for in You do I trust;
cause me to know the way in which I
should walk, for I lift up my soul to You.*
— PSALM 143:8 —

Prayer Notes

_____

_____

_____

_____

_____

_____

_____

_____

_____

_____

_____

_____

Her Protection

Lord, I pray that You would surround (wife's name) with Your hand of protection. Keep her safe from any accidents, diseases, or evil influences. Protect her in cars, planes, or wherever she is. Keep her out of harm's way. Let no weapon formed against my wife be able to prosper (Isaiah 54:17). Shield her from the plans of evil people. Thank You, Lord, that this day You will cover (wife's name) and will help her to lie down in peace, and sleep; for You alone, O Lord, make her to dwell in safety (Psalm 4:8).

The LORD is my rock and my fortress and my deliverer; my God, my strength, in whom I will trust; my shield and the horn of my salvation, my stronghold. I will call upon the LORD, who is worthy to be praised; so shall I be saved from my enemies.

— PSALM 18:2-3 —

Prayer Notes

_____
_____
_____
_____
_____
_____
_____
_____
_____
_____
_____
_____
_____

Her Protection

Lord, I pray that You would help (wife's name) to truly see that her body is Your dwelling place. Enable her to protect her body through right choices in what she eats. Give her the motivation to exercise regularly so that she has endurance. Help her to get plenty of rest so that she is completely rejuvenated when she awakens. May she acknowledge You in all her ways—including the care of her body—so that You can direct her paths. Watch over her as she moves through her day and performs the tasks that demand her time and attention.

You were bought at a price; therefore glorify God in your body and in your spirit, which are God's.

— 1 Corinthians 6:20 —

Prayer Notes

_____

_____

_____

_____

_____

_____

_____

_____

_____

_____

_____

_____

_____

_____

_____

Her Protection

Lord, give Your angels charge over (wife's name) to keep her in all her ways (Psalm 91:11). I say to my wife that God will "cover you with His feathers, and under His wings you shall take refuge; His truth shall be your shield and buckler. You shall not be afraid of the terror by night, nor of the arrow that flies by day, nor of the pestilence that walks in darkness, nor of the destruction that lays waste at noonday. A thousand may fall at your side, and ten thousand at your right hand; but it shall not come near you" (Psalm 91:4-7).

The angel of the LORD encamps all around
those who fear Him, and delivers them.

— PSALM 34:7 —

Prayer Notes

_____

_____

_____

_____

_____

_____

_____

_____

_____

_____

_____

_____

_____

_____

_____

Her Desires

Lord, I pray that You would touch (wife's name) this day and fulfill her deepest desires. In the midst of all she has to do, let there be ample time for what she enjoys most. Help her to surrender her dreams to You so that You can bring to life the ones You have placed in her heart. I pray that she will never try to follow a dream of her own making, one that You will not bless. Help her to surrender *her* plans so that You can reveal *Your* plan. I know that in Your plan, timing is everything. May she reach for her highest dreams in Your perfect timing.

He will fulfill the desire of those who fear Him;
He also will hear their cry and save them.

— PSALM 145:19 —

Prayer Notes

_____

_____

_____

_____

_____

_____

_____

_____

_____

_____

_____

_____

_____

_____

_____

Her Desires

Lord, help me understand the things that interest (wife's name). I also pray that You would make a way for us to share (name a specific activity or interest you would like to do together). Help her to understand my enjoyment of it, and may she develop an appreciation for it too. I know that You would not give us dreams that aren't compatible. I pray that the desires of our hearts will be perfectly knitted together. May we not only be caught up in our own dreams but in each other's as well. Help us to always share with one another the deepest desires of our hearts.

*You open Your hand and satisfy
the desire of every living thing.*

— PSALM 145:16 —

Prayer Notes

_____

_____

_____

_____

_____

_____

_____

_____

_____

_____

_____

_____

_____

_____

Her Work

Lord, I pray that You would help (wife's name) to be successful in her work. No matter what her work is at any given time, establish it and help her to find favor through it. Thank You for the abilities, gifts, and creativity You have placed in her. Continue to reveal, develop, and refine those gifts and talents, and use them for Your purposes. May her skills increase in value, and may she excel in each of them. Open doors for her that no man can shut, and bless her with success. Give her the gift of work that she loves and establish the work of her hands (Psalm 90:17).

The labor of the righteous leads to life.

— PROVERBS 10:16 —

Prayer Notes

_____

_____

_____

_____

_____

_____

_____

_____

_____

_____

_____

_____

_____

_____

Her Work

Lord, I pray that You would keep my wife and me from ever being in competition with one another, and help us to always rejoice in each other's accomplishments. Help us to build one another up and not forget that we are on the same team. Show me how I can encourage (wife's name). Lord, Your Word says when we commit our work to You, the financial blessing we receive will not bring misery along with it (Proverbs 10:22). You have also said "the laborer is worthy of his wages" (1 Timothy 5:18). I pray that (wife's name) will be rewarded well for her labor and that it will bless her, our family, and others.

*Give her of the fruit of her hands, and
let her own works praise her in the gates.*

— Proverbs 31:31 —

Prayer Notes

_____

_____

_____

_____

_____

_____

_____

_____

_____

_____

_____

_____

_____

Her Deliverance

Lord, I pray that You would set (wife's name) free from anything that holds her other than You. Deliver her from any memory of the past that has the power to control her or keep her trapped in its grip. Help her to forgive any person who has hurt her so that unforgiveness will not be able to hold her captive. Set her free from everything that keeps her from being all You created her to be. Keep her protected from the plans of the enemy so that he cannot thwart the deliverance and healing You want to bring about in her life.

*Do not remember the former things, nor
consider the things of old. Behold, I will
do a new thing, now it shall spring forth;
shall you not know it? I will even make a
road in the wilderness and rivers in the desert.*

— ISAIAH 43:18-19 —

Prayer Notes

_____

_____

_____

_____

_____

_____

_____

_____

_____

_____

_____

Her Deliverance

*L*ord, I ask that You would restore all that has ever been stolen from (wife's name) until she is lacking no good thing. I know that in Your presence is healing and wholeness. Help (wife's name) to live in Your presence so that she can be made totally whole. I know that "though we walk in the flesh, we do not war according to the flesh. For the weapons of our warfare are not carnal but mighty in God for pulling down strongholds" (2 Corinthians 10:3-4). In the name of Jesus I pull down any strongholds the enemy has erected around (wife's name).

The Lord will deliver me from every evil work and preserve me for His heavenly kingdom. To Him be glory forever and ever.

— 2 TIMOTHY 4:18 —

Prayer Notes

_____

_____

_____

_____

_____

_____

_____

_____

_____

_____

_____

_____

_____

_____

Her Deliverance

Lord, today I pray that (wife's name) will find freedom from (name a specific area of struggle from which your wife needs to find freedom). Set her free from this in the name of Jesus. I pray that for her sake You "will not rest, until her righteousness goes forth as brightness, and her salvation as a lamp that burns" (Isaiah 62:1). Make darkness light before her "and crooked places straight" (Isaiah 42:16). You have said in Your Word that "whoever walks wisely will be delivered" (Proverbs 28:26). I pray she will walk with wisdom and find full deliverance. Show me how to love and support her well in the process.

*If anyone is in Christ, he is a new
creation; old things have passed away;
behold, all things have become new.*

— 2 CORINTHIANS 5:17 —

Prayer Notes

Her Obedience

Lord, I pray that You would enable (wife's name) to live in total obedience to Your laws and Your ways. Help her to see where her thoughts and actions are not lined up with Your directions as to how she is to live. Keep my wife from doing anything that separates her from the fullness of Your presence and Your love. Help her to hear Your instructions, and give her the desire to do what You ask. Remind her to confess any error quickly, and enable her to take the steps of obedience she needs to take. Show her where she is not living in obedience, and help her to do what she needs to do.

If they obey and serve Him, they shall spend their days in prosperity, and their years in pleasures.

— JOB 36:11 —

Prayer Notes

_____

_____

_____

_____

_____

_____

_____

_____

_____

_____

_____

_____

_____

_____

Her Obedience

Lord, Your Word says, "He who obeys instruction guards his life" (Proverbs 19:16 NIV). Bless my wife's mind, emotions, and will as she takes steps of obedience. Your Word also says that "out of the overflow of the heart the mouth speaks" (Matthew 12:34 NIV). Fill my wife's heart with Your love, peace, and joy this day so that the sweetness of Your presence within her overflows in her words. May Your Spirit control her tongue so that everything she speaks brings life. Help (wife's name) to say as David did, "I have resolved that my mouth will not sin" (Psalm 17:3 NIV).

*Do not forget my law, but let your heart
keep my commands; for length of days and
long life and peace they will add to you.*

— PROVERBS 3:1-2 —

Prayer Notes

_____

_____

_____

_____

_____

_____

_____

_____

_____

_____

_____

_____

_____

Her Obedience

Lord, Your Word says, "No good thing will He withhold from those who walk uprightly" (Psalm 84:11). I pray that (wife's name) will walk uprightly and that You will pour out Your blessings upon her. Especially bless her with the peace and long life You speak of in Your Word (Proverbs 3:1-2). I pray this day that my wife will walk in obedience to You and that You will reward her with an abundance of good things. Let the words of her mouth and the meditation of her heart be always acceptable in Your sight, O Lord, our strength and our Redeemer (Psalm 19:14).

The path of the just is like the shining sun,
that shines ever brighter unto the perfect day.

— PROVERBS 4:18 —

Prayer Notes

_____

_____

_____

_____

_____

_____

_____

_____

_____

_____

_____

_____

_____

_____

_____

Her Future

Lord, I pray for (wife's name) to have total peace about the past, present, and future of her life. Give her a vision for her future that makes her certain she is safe in Your hands. Free her completely from the past so that nothing interferes with the future You have for her. Help her to see her future from Your perspective and not believe any lies of the enemy about it. May she trust Your promise that the plans You have for her are for good and not evil, to give her a future and a hope (Jeremiah 29:11 NIV).

Eye has not seen, nor ear heard, nor have
entered into the heart of man the things which
God has prepared for those who love Him.
– 1 Corinthians 2:9 –

Prayer Notes

_____

_____

_____

_____

_____

_____

_____

_____

_____

_____

_____

_____

_____

Her Future

Lord, I pray that You would give (wife's name) wisdom in all things now and in the days to come. Give her confidence that the future is something she never has to fear. Give her wisdom in her work, travels, relationships, and finances. Bless her with the discernment to distinguish the truth from a lie. May she have the contentment, longevity, enjoyment, vitality, riches, and happiness that Your Word says are there for those who find wisdom (Proverbs 3:16-18). May she also find protection, grace, rest, freedom from fear, and confidence in You (Proverbs 3:21-26).

*There is surely a future hope for you,
and your hope will not be cut off.*

— PROVERBS 23:18 (NIV) —

Prayer Notes

_____
_____
_____
_____
_____
_____
_____
_____
_____
_____
_____
_____
_____
_____

Her Future

Lord, I ask that You would take (wife's name) from glory to glory and strength to strength as she learns to depend on Your wisdom and not lean on her own understanding. When she needs to make any decision, I pray that You, Holy Spirit, will guide her. For the decisions we make together, give us wisdom to make them in unity. Specifically I pray for (name a decision you must make together). Help us to know Your will in this matter. I pray that we will make godly choices and decisions that are pleasing to You.

When He, the Spirit of truth, has come, He will guide you into all truth.
— JOHN 16:13 —

Prayer Notes

Her Future

Lord, I pray that (wife's name) will be planted in Your house and flourish in Your courts. May the fruit of her life be seen every year, and even into old age may she be fresh and flourishing (Psalm 92:13-14). Bless her with long life, and when she comes to the end of her life, may it not be one moment before Your chosen time. Let that transition also be attended with peace and joy, and the absence of suffering. Let it be said of her that she was Your light to the world around her.

For I know the thoughts I think toward
you, says the LORD, thoughts of peace and
not of evil, to give you a future and a hope.
— JEREMIAH 29:11 —

Prayer Notes

_____

_____

_____

_____

_____

_____

_____

_____

_____

_____

_____

_____

_____

The Power
of PRAYER™
to Change Your
MARRIAGE
BOOK OF PRAYERS

STORMIE
OMARTIAN

HARVEST HOUSE PUBLISHERS

EUGENE, OREGON

THE POWER OF PRAYER™ TO CHANGE YOUR MARRIAGE BOOK OF PRAYERS
Copyright © 2009 by Stormie Omartian
Published by Harvest House Publishers
Eugene, Oregon 97402
www.harvesthousepublishers.com

ISBN 978-0-7369-2054-4

Introduction

Whether you want to *protect* your marriage from the things that can damage or destroy it, or you long to *mend* and *restore* your relationship where it has been broken or hurt, or you desire to bring peace and unity where there has been strife, the prayers in this book are for you. There is a way to pray about the deeper issues of marriage that can either help you avoid them or enable you to see redemption come where a problem already exists. God has given *you* authority to pray for your husband or wife and invite the power of God to work in his or her life and in your lives together, as well as your own life personally.

It is my hope for you that each and every prayer in this book will be a starting point from which you will be inspired to continue on praying about the specifics of your own marriage. When you *pray powerfully* for your relationship, you will see God *work powerfully* in it. You will see *God do miracles* when you pray to the *God of miracles*, believing that He hears you and will answer. It happened in my life, and I am certain it can happen in yours. If you don't give up, your faith-filled prayers can strengthen your marriage so that it will last a lifetime.

Stormie Omartian

Whatever things you ask in prayer,
believing, you will receive.

MATTHEW 21:22

1

If Communication Breaks Down

LORD, I pray You would protect my husband (wife) and me from any kind of breakdown of communication. Enable us to always share our thoughts and feelings and refuse to be people who don't talk. Teach us to trust each other enough to share our deepest hopes, dreams, fears, and struggles with one another. Help us to spend time communicating with *You* every day so that our communication with each other will always be good. Teach us how to openly express love for one another, and keep us from any laziness or selfishness that would cause us to neglect to do that. Help us to refuse to speak words that tear down, but only words that build up (Ephesians 4:29).

*Let the words of my mouth and the meditation
of my heart be acceptable in Your sight, O LORD,
my strength and my Redeemer.*

PSALM 19:14

PRAYER NOTES

2

If Communication Breaks Down

LORD, teach us to listen to one another and recognize the signs in each other that give us greater understanding. Help us find things we enjoy doing together so that we will grow closer and not apart. Enable us to be able to communicate love, appreciation, and honor to each other at all times. Help us to take instant authority over any attack the enemy brings against us—especially in the area of communication. Help us to settle all matters of disagreement between us in a loving, compromising, and considerate manner. Enable us to always be in unity with You and with each other.

Bear with each other and forgive whatever grievances you may have against one another. Forgive as the Lord forgave you. And over all these virtues put on love, which binds them all together in perfect unity.

COLOSSIANS 3:13-14 NIV

PRAYER NOTES

3

If Communication Breaks Down

LORD, I need to be changed. Reveal any times where I have not said the right words or communicated the right things to my husband (wife) and I will confess it as sin, for I know I fall far short of Your glory (Romans 3:23). Teach me how to communicate openly and honestly so I will speak excellent, right, and truthful words (Proverbs 8:6-9). Take away any deceit in my heart and any perversity in my mind so that evil will be far from me (Proverbs 17:20). I pray that Your love will be so much in my heart that it comes out in everything I say. Give me the right words for every situation.

We all stumble in many things.
If anyone does not stumble in word, he is a perfect
man, able also to bridle the whole body.

JAMES 3:2

PRAYER NOTES

_____

_____

_____

_____

_____

_____

_____

4

If Communication Breaks Down

LORD, I pray You would open my husband's (wife's) heart to all You have for him (her) and for our marriage together. Help him (her) to know You better, to understand Your ways, and to see things from Your perspective. Help him (her) to view the two of us the way You do. Make changes in him (her) that need to be made so that nothing will hinder him (her) from fulfilling the purpose and destiny You have for his (her) life and our lives together. Lord, fill my husband's (wife's) heart with Your love so that it overflows in the words he (she) speaks. Help us to be instruments of Your peace and grace every time we speak to each other.

Husbands ought to love their own wives as their own bodies; he who loves his wife loves himself...and let the wife see that she respects her husband.

EPHESIANS 5:28,33

PRAYER NOTES

5

If Communication Breaks Down

LORD, give me ears to really hear what my husband (wife) is saying so that I can bear some of his (her) burdens by simply listening. Make me quick to hear and slow to speak (James 1:19). Give me the wisdom to have a good sense of timing. I pray that "my mouth shall speak wisdom, and the meditation of my heart shall give understanding" (Psalm 49:3). May there be no division between us because we are of the same mind and have the same good judgment (1 Corinthians 1:10). Where either of us has not communicated well in the past, help us to do so now. Thank You that You are our rock and our Redeemer, and You can redeem all things (Psalm 78:35).

For your Maker is your husband, the LORD of hosts is His name; and your Redeemer is the Holy One of Israel; He is called the God of the whole earth.

ISAIAH 54:5

PRAYER NOTES

_____

_____

_____

_____

_____

_____

_____

6

If Anger, Rudeness, or Abuse Poisons Your Relationship

LORD, keep us from ever using anger as a weapon to hurt one another so that it doesn't drive a wedge between us. Fill our hearts full of Your love and peace so there is no room for anger. Teach us to pray about everything and make all of our needs known to You, knowing that when we do You have promised in Your Word to give us Your peace (Philippians 4:6-7). Lord, enable us to always see the best in one another and not the worst. Teach us to find things to praise about each other and not complain about, so that we can be brought into harmony with You and each other in our marriage (Philippians 4:8-9).

Be angry, and do not sin.
Meditate within your heart
on your bed, and be still.

PSALM 4:4

PRAYER NOTES

_____

_____

_____

_____

_____

_____

7

If Anger, Rudeness, or Abuse Poisons Your Relationship

LORD, help my husband (wife) and me to always "pursue the things which make for peace" and the things by which we may edify one another (Romans 14:19). Enable us to exhibit the fruit of the Spirit—"love, joy, peace, longsuffering, kindness, goodness, faithfulness, gentleness, self-control"—and not a harvest of the flesh (Galatians 5:22-23). Take all anger from us and teach us to love each other from pure hearts and a good conscience (1 Timothy 1:5-6). We know that it is You who "looks deep inside people and searches through their thoughts" (Proverbs 20:27 NCV). Search the inner depths of our hearts and expose anything that is not of You so that we can be free of it.

*Let every man be swift to hear,
slow to speak, slow to wrath; for the wrath of man
does not produce the righteousness of God.*

JAMES 1:19-20

PRAYER NOTES

_____

_____

_____

_____

_____

_____

_____

8

If Anger, Rudeness, or Abuse Poisons Your Relationship

LORD, where I have directed anger toward my husband (wife) or held anger inside of me, I confess that as sin and ask You to forgive me and take all anger away. Heal any wounds I have inflicted on him (her) with my words. Help me to speak good words and healing to my husband (wife), for I know that pleases You (Proverbs 15:23). Where I have shown anger toward any other family member, I confess it to You as sin. Bring Your restoration to every situation where it is needed. Thank You that You will take away all anger in me and keep me in perfect peace, because my mind is fixed on You (Isaiah 26:3).

Above all things have fervent love for one another,
for love will cover a multitude of sins.

1 PETER 4:8

PRAYER NOTES

9

If Anger, Rudeness, or Abuse Poisons Your Relationship

⁓

LORD, help my husband (wife) to understand that anger never produces spiritual fruit (James 1:20). I pray that all anger in him (her) will be evaporated by the power of the Holy Spirit. I pray now that You, the God of all hope, will fill my husband (wife) with faith and hope by the power of the Holy Spirit (Romans 15:13). I pray You would lift up Your countenance upon him (her) and give him (her) Your peace (Numbers 6:26). I pray that You would direct his (her) heart "into the love of God and into the patience of Christ" (2 Thessalonians 3:5). Help him (her) to flee anger and pursue righteousness, godliness, faith, love, patience, and gentleness (1 Timothy 6:11).

Cease from anger, and forsake wrath;
do not fret—it only causes harm.
For evildoers shall be cut off; but those who wait on
*the L*ORD*, they shall inherit the earth.*

PSALM 37:8-9

PRAYER NOTES

_____

_____

_____

_____

_____

_____

_____

10

If Forgiveness Doesn't Come Easy

LORD, I pray You would help my husband (wife) and me to always be completely forgiving of one another. Please give each of us a heart to forgive freely—whether the other asks for it or not. Help us both to "grow in the grace and knowledge of our Lord and Savior Jesus Christ" (2 Peter 3:18), so that we will become forgiving the way You are. Help us to forgive so that we will be forgiven (Luke 6:37). Help us to love one another the way You love us, so that letting go of offenses will be easy. Help us to be merciful to one another, because we have Your goodness and mercy following us as You promised in Your Word (Psalm 23:6).

Whenever you stand praying, if you have anything
against anyone, forgive him that your Father in
heaven may also forgive you your trespasses.

MARK 11:25

PRAYER NOTES

If Forgiveness
Doesn't Come Easy

THANK YOU, Lord, that I can do *all* things through Christ who strengthens me, and therefore I have the strength to forgive my husband (wife) for anything that has hurt or disappointed me. Thank You that You are the God of forgiveness. Thank You for Your mercy and grace to me. Thank You that You have released me from any stronghold of unforgiveness. Take away any feelings in me that cause me to think I need to pay back hurt for hurt. I "strive to have a conscience without offense" toward You or my husband (wife) (Acts 24:16). Where I need to be forgiven, help me to apologize and receive forgiveness from my husband (wife).

*Be submissive to one another,
and be clothed with humility, for God resists the
proud, but gives grace to the humble.*

1 Peter 5:5

Prayer Notes

12

If Forgiveness
Doesn't Come Easy

LORD, I know there are places in me that harbor unforgiveness that I am not even aware of. Please reveal those to me so I can confess them to You. For "You, Lord, are good, and ready to forgive, and abundant in mercy to all those who call upon You" (Psalm 86:5). I ask You to forgive me for any unforgiveness I have toward anyone, especially my husband (wife). I know that You, Lord, are the only one who knows the whole story, so I refuse to be the judge of all that happens in my husband (wife). You are the one "who will both bring to light the hidden things of darkness and reveal the counsels of the [heart]" (1 Corinthians 4:5).

Confess your trespasses to one another, and pray for one another, that you may be healed. The effective, fervent prayer of a righteous man avails much.

JAMES 5:16

PRAYER NOTES

_____

_____

_____

_____

_____

_____

_____

13

If Forgiveness Doesn't Come Easy

LORD, I lift my husband (wife) to You in prayer and ask You to help him (her) let go of any unforgiveness that he (she) harbors. Help him (her) to forgive me for anything I have done—or *not* done—that was displeasing to him (her). I pray that You, "the God of patience and comfort," will grant to my husband (wife) the ability to be "like-minded" toward me so that we together may glorify You with a single-minded voice of unity (Romans 15:5-6). Give him (her) a heart of mercy toward me so that he (she) can truly let go of anything I have said or done that has hurt him (her).

If there is any consolation in Christ, if any comfort of love, if any fellowship of the Spirit, if any affection and mercy, fulfill my joy by being like-minded, having the same love, being of one accord, of one mind.

PHILIPPIANS 2:1-2

PRAYER NOTES

_____

_____

_____

_____

_____

_____

_____

14

If Depression or Negative Emotions Spoil the Atmosphere

LORD, I thank You that You show us the paths of life and "in Your presence is fullness of joy; at Your right hand are pleasures forevermore" (Psalm 16:11). Thank You that when we delight ourselves in You, You will cause us "to ride on the high hills of the earth" (Isaiah 58:14). I pray that You will keep my husband (wife) and me from all negative emotions. Help us to see that we never have to live with any of them. Where we have allowed anything such as depression, anxiety, fear, rejection, or loneliness to influence our lives, deliver us out of all that and keep it far from us.

You are my hiding place;
You shall preserve me from trouble;
You shall surround me
with songs of deliverance.

PSALM 32:7

PRAYER NOTES

_____

_____

_____

_____

_____

_____

_____

15

If Depression or Negative Emotions Spoil the Atmosphere

LORD, I pray that even though my husband (wife) and I may go through times where we are hard-pressed on every side, we will not be crushed, nor will we be in despair (2 Corinthians 4:8). We will rejoice in Your Word and the comfort of Your presence. We will not forget that You have the power to set us free. Your commandments are right and they make our hearts rejoice (Psalm 19:8). We were once in darkness, but now we are in Your light. Help us to always "walk as children of the light" (Ephesians 5:8). I pray we will always look to You and put our hope and expectations in You (Psalm 62:5).

He has delivered us from the power of darkness and conveyed us into the kingdom of the Son of His love.

COLOSSIANS 1:13

PRAYER NOTES

16

If Depression or Negative Emotions Spoil the Atmosphere

LORD, wherever I have allowed negative emotions to control me, deliver me forever from them. Show me things in my life that have been passed down in my family—attitudes, fears, prejudices, and even depression—and break these strongholds completely. Keep me from falling into habits of the heart that are learned responses to life. Lord, I pray for healing and deliverance from any depression, anxiety, fear, rejection, loneliness, or any other negative emotion that would seek to find permanent residence in my heart. You are the lamp of my soul, Lord, and I thank You that You "will enlighten my darkness" (Psalm 18:28). Thank You that You will give me rest from my sorrow and fear (Isaiah 14:3).

He shall cover you with His feathers,
and under His wings you shall take refuge;
His truth shall be your shield and buckler.

PSALM 91:4

PRAYER NOTES

_____

_____

_____

_____

_____

_____

17

If Depression or Negative Emotions Spoil the Atmosphere

—⁓—

LORD, take away all sadness or despair. Heal the hurt in my heart. Give me a garment of praise at all times and take away the spirit of heaviness. Make me to be a tree of strength. Plant me and feed me in Your Word so that Your glory will be revealed in me. Rebuild the places in me that have been damaged or ruined in the past. Lord, I pray that You would "send out Your light and Your truth! Let them lead me; let them bring me to Your holy hill and to Your tabernacle" (Psalm 43:3). May Your light in my life completely evaporate any black clouds around me so that they cannot keep me from sensing Your presence in my life.

*He has sent Me to heal the brokenhearted…to give
them beauty for ashes, the oil of joy for mourning,
the garment of praise for the spirit of heaviness; that
they may be called trees of righteousness, the planting
of the LORD, that He may be glorified.*

Isaiah 61:1,3

Prayer Notes

18

If Depression or Negative Emotions Spoil the Atmosphere

———— ✦ ————

LORD, thank You for Your promise to bring out Your "people with joy" and Your "chosen ones with gladness" (Psalm 105:43). Thank You that because of You, "darkness is passing away, and the true light is already shining" in my husband's (wife's) life (1 John 2:8). Help him (her) to keep his (her) eyes on You and take refuge in You knowing that You will not leave his (her) soul destitute (Psalm 141:8). Have mercy on him (her) and be his (her) helper! (Psalm 30:10). Anoint him (her) with Your "oil of gladness" (Psalm 45:7). Restore to him (her) the joy of Your salvation, and uphold him (her) "by Your generous Spirit" (Psalm 51:12). Set him (her) free from anything that holds him (her) other than You.

You shall know the truth,
and the truth shall make you free.

JOHN 8:32

PRAYER NOTES

_____

_____

_____

_____

_____

_____

_____

19

If Children Start to Dominate Your Lives

LORD, help us to learn how to pray for marriage and our children so that we never leave any aspect of our lives or their lives to chance. Your Word says that "unless the LORD builds the house, they labor in vain who build it" (Psalm 127:1). So I invite You right now to build and establish our house, our family, and our marriage. I pray that we will never be divided or torn apart. Give me and my husband (wife) great wisdom and revelation about how to raise our children. Help us to talk things through and be in complete unity, especially in the area of discipline and privileges. Show us what we need to see about ourselves and each child.

He has strengthened the bars of your gates;
He has blessed your children within you.

PRAYER NOTES

20

If Children Start to Dominate Your Lives

———

LORD, help me to be balanced in my parenting. Help me to not be obsessive about my children, but rather to relinquish control over their lives to You. Help me to find the balance between focusing too much on my children and neglecting my husband (wife), and the other extreme of neglecting my children in any way. Help me to put You first and my husband (wife) second in my life, so that my focus on our children doesn't come between those two relationships. Wherever there are disagreements between me and my husband (wife) as to how to raise and discipline our children, help us to be able to communicate well with each other and resolve whatever conflict we have.

The righteous man walks in his integrity;
his children are blessed after him.

PROVERBS 20:7

PRAYER NOTES

_____

_____

_____

_____

_____

_____

_____

If Children Start to Dominate Your Lives

LORD, give me Your wisdom, revelation, and discernment. Give me Your strength, patience, and love. Teach me how to truly intercede for my children without trying to impose my own will when I pray. Teach me how to pray so I can lay the burden of raising them at Your feet. Increase my faith to believe for all the things You put on my heart to pray about for them. Lord, I know that I don't have the ability to be the perfect parent, but *You* do. I pray that You would protect and guide them. Help me not to live in fear about my children because of all possible dangers, but to live in peace trusting that You are in control.

All your children shall be taught by the LORD,
and great shall be the peace of your children.

ISAIAH 54:13

PRAYER NOTES

_____

_____

_____

_____

_____

_____

_____

22

If Children Start to Dominate Your Lives

LORD, I pray for my husband (wife) to find the perfect balance between being overly focused on the children and the other extreme of not spending enough time with them. Let no issues of child rearing change his (her) heart toward me or undermine our relationship. Help him (her) to see the need for us to spend time together alone so that we can stay strong and connected as a married couple. Help my husband (wife) to obey You and do what is right in Your sight so that his (her) prayers will be answered—especially for our children. Give him (her) wisdom and revelation about all aspects of child rearing and help him (her) to be a great father (mother) to our children.

*May the LORD give you increase more
and more, you and your children.*

PSALM 115:14

PRAYER NOTES

_____

_____

_____

_____

_____

_____

23

If Finances Get Out of Control

LORD, help my husband (wife) and me to remember that it is You who gives us the ability to produce wealth (Deuteronomy 8:18). That the earth is Yours and everything in it belongs to You (Psalm 24:1). That You, Lord, own every animal and creature and "the cattle on a thousand hills" (Psalm 50:10-11). Everything we have comes from You, so help us to be good stewards of our finances. Help us to be calm and wise in handling money so that we may prosper and not make hasty, rash, or impulsive decisions (Proverbs 21:5). Help us to work diligently, to be content with what we have, and to learn to give (Proverbs 21:25-26).

The LORD will open to you His good treasure, the heavens, to give the rain to your land in its season, and to bless all the work of your hand.

DEUTERONOMY 28:12

PRAYER NOTES

24

If Finances Get Out of Control

LORD, I know that having good health, a loving and supportive family, a solid marriage, great friends, good and satisfying work, and a sense of purpose in helping others is the richest life of all. Help us to always put our sights on those clear priorities. Lord, I pray that You would bless us with provision and help us to always be wise in the decisions we make regarding our spending. Give us the wisdom and the courage to resist spending foolishly. Help us to tithe and give offerings to You, and show us how you would have us give to others. Help my husband (wife) and me to completely agree on our spending as well as our giving.

The LORD your God will make you
abound in all the work of your hand.

DEUTERONOMY 30:9

PRAYER NOTES

_____

_____

_____

_____

_____

_____

25

If Finances Get Out of Control

LORD, I pray that You will give me wisdom with money. Help me to generate it and spend it wisely. Help me to give according to Your will and ways. Show me when I am tempted to buy something I don't need or will regret later. Help me to avoid certain places that are traps for me, where I will be tempted to spend foolishly. Help me not to be drawn toward things that will not add to our lives. I submit our finances to You and ask that You would reveal to me all that I should know or do. I don't want to look back in regret but look forward to a secure future.

Oh, taste and see that the LORD is good;
blessed is the man who trusts in Him!

PSALM 34:8

PRAYER NOTES

_____

_____

_____

_____

_____

_____

_____

26

If Finances Get
Out of Control

LORD, I pray that You would give my spouse wisdom about our finances. Help him (her) to trust You with all his (her) heart and not depend on his (her) own understanding (Proverbs 3:5). Help him (her) to not be wise in his (her) own eyes, but to fear You and stay far from evil (Proverbs 3:7). Give him (her) a good business sense and the ability to be responsible with money. Show him (her) insight into Your truth and give him (her) the power to resist temptation when it comes to needless spending. Where he (she) has made mistakes with money, I pray that You would reveal Your truth to him (her).

He who is faithful in what is least
is faithful also in much.

Luke 16:10

Prayer Notes

_____

_____

_____

_____

_____

_____

_____

27

If Finances Get Out of Control

LORD, I ask that You would establish the work of my husband's (wife's) hands (Psalm 90:17). Help him (her) to know that "there is nothing too hard for You" (Jeremiah 32:17). Help him (her) to know that even though there are times when he (she) is not seeing the desired fruit of his (her) labor now, that he (she) can still rejoice and say, "The LORD God is my strength; He will make my feet like deer's feet, and He will make me walk on my high hills" (Habakkuk 3:19). I know that we must not trust in uncertain riches but in You, for it is You "who gives us richly all things to enjoy" (1 Timothy 6:17).

The God of heaven Himself will prosper us.

NEHEMIAH 2:20

PRAYER NOTES

28

If Addictions or Other Destructive Behaviors Manifest

LORD, I pray that You would protect my husband (wife) and me from any kind of self-destructive behavior. Open our eyes to see if we have allowed habits into our lives that have the potential to harm us. Bring to light all things. Where we have opened ourselves up to bad or destructive habits, help us to get free. Give us the ability to cope with any frustration or anxiety we may have by taking all concerns to You and each other and not looking for relief from outside resources. Lord, You have promised that "if we confess our sins" You are "faithful and just to forgive us our sins and to cleanse us from all unrighteousness" (1 John 1:9).

*Being confident of this very thing,
that He who has begun a good work in you
will complete it until the day of Jesus Christ.*

PHILIPPIANS 1:6

PRAYER NOTES

29

If Addictions or Other Destructive Behaviors Manifest

LORD, I pray that You would reveal to me any destructive habit I have embraced and help me to fully understand why I do it. Help me to truly see how it is not Your will for my life. Break any spirit of rebellion in me that causes me to feel that I can do what I want, when I want, without regard for the consequences. Enable me to see how what I do affects my husband (wife) and family. Where You or other people—especially my husband (wife) or children—have tried to warn me, give me ears to hear. Bring me to complete repentance before You and them for ever ignoring those warnings.

All things are lawful for me, but all things are not helpful. All things are lawful for me, but I will not be brought under the power of any.

1 CORINTHIANS 6:12

PRAYER NOTES

30

If Addictions or Other Destructive Behaviors Manifest

LORD, help me not to hold resentment toward anyone who tries to confront me on any problem, especially my husband (wife). Enable me to remember that "open rebuke is better than love carefully concealed" and "faithful are the wounds of a friend" (Proverbs 27:5-6). I know that "You desire truth in the inward parts, and in the hidden part You will make me to know wisdom" (Psalm 51:6). Help me to become a person of truth who does not have a secret life. Thank You, Jesus, that You are my healer. You are my refuge and strength, a very present help in times of trouble (Psalm 46:1). Thank You, God, that you are my Comforter and Helper.

*My brethren, be strong in the Lord
and in the power of His might. Put on the
whole armor of God, that you may be able
to stand against the wiles of the devil.*

EPHESIANS 6:10-11

PRAYER NOTES

31

If Addictions or Other Destructive Behaviors Manifest

LORD, I pray that my husband (wife) will have eyes to see the truth and ears to hear Your voice speaking to him (her). May Your will be done in his (her) life. I release him (her) to You and ask You to set him (her) free from any destructive habits. I fully realize that I can't control the situation, nor do I even want to. I give up any need to try and fix things or take control of the problem. I give up any desire to make my husband (wife) change. I release him (her) into Your hands and ask You to do what it takes to make the changes You want in him (her).

*Do not be conformed to this world,
but be transformed by the renewing of your mind,
that you may prove what is that good
and acceptable and perfect will of God.*

ROMANS 12:2

PRAYER NOTES

_____

_____

_____

_____

_____

_____

32

If Addictions or Other Destructive Behaviors Manifest

LORD, help my husband (wife) face all problems and view them as something that can be overcome and not something insurmountable. Enable him (her) to take responsibility for his (her) actions and not live in denial about them. Help him (her) to take responsibility for his (her) own life and not blame others for things that have happened. I pray that he (she) will always be completely honest with me about everything he (she) is doing. Tear down any walls that have been erected between us. Help him (her) to understand his (her) worth in Your sight. Help him (her) to seek You as his (her) healer and deliverer, so he (she) can find total restoration in You.

Restore to me the joy of Your salvation,
and uphold me by Your generous Spirit.

PSALM 51:12

PRAYER NOTES

_____

_____

_____

_____

_____

_____

_____

33

If Outside Influences Pollute Your Sexual Relationship

LORD, I pray You would bless our marriage in every way and specifically protect our sexual relationship. Help us to always put each other first and never sacrifice one another out of selfish disregard for the other's needs. Keep our eyes from looking at anything that would compromise our relationship. Keep our hearts from being enticed and drawn away from each other. Help us to walk properly and not in lust or strife (Romans 13:13). Enable us to always live in the Spirit so we don't fulfill the lust of the flesh (Galatians 5:16). Open our eyes to recognize ungodliness and worldliness so that we can reject those enticements and learn to live Your way.

How can a young man cleanse his way? By taking heed according to Your Word. With my whole heart I have sought You; oh, let me not wander from Your commandments! Your word I have hidden in my heart, that I might not sin against You.

PSALM 119:9-11

PRAYER NOTES

_____

_____

_____

_____

_____

_____

34

If Outside Influences Pollute Your Sexual Relationship

LORD, I pray You would make me the wife (husband) You want me to be. Help me to fulfill my husband (wife) sexually. Teach me how to be attentive to his (her) needs and desires, and to put his (her) needs before my own. Please help me to be a wife (husband) who is faithful and true in thought and deed. Help us both to become so committed to You that nothing else matters to us more than living in obedience to Your ways. Enable us to see things from Your perspective. Expose all of our sins to Your light so that neither of us can have a secret life. Reveal everything in either of us that needs to be seen.

When wisdom enters your heart,
and knowledge is pleasant to your soul,
discretion will preserve you; understanding will
keep you, to deliver you from the way of evil.

PROVERBS 2:10-12

PRAYER NOTES

35

If Outside Influences Pollute Your Sexual Relationship

LORD, I lift my eyes up to You in heaven and deliberately take them off the things of earth (Psalm 123:1). I take comfort in the fact that You are my refuge that I can go to any time I am tempted to look at anything ungodly, or see in my mind that which does not please You (Psalm 141:8). Take away all that is in me that holds the door open for sinful and lustful thoughts. Help me to be a wife (husband) who is faithful and true in thought and deed. "O LORD, You have searched me and known me...You understand my thought afar off" (Psalm 139:1-2). "Show me Your ways, O LORD...on You I wait all the day" (Psalm 25:4-5).

Those who are of a perverse heart are an abomination to the LORD, but the blameless in their ways are His delight.

PROVERBS 11:20

PRAYER NOTES

36

If Outside Influences Pollute Your Sexual Relationship

LORD, I surrender my husband (wife) to You completely. Do whatever it takes to get him (her) to see the truth about all that he (she) does. Put Your love in his (her) heart for me, and keep his (her) eyes, heart, and mind from finding others attractive. Expose every lie masquerading as truth to him (her). Help him (her) to put off all conduct that is not in alignment with Your will and reject all corruption that comes from "deceitful lusts" (Ephesians 4:22). Don't let him (her) be taken down a path that leads to death and hell (Proverbs 5:3-5). Deliver him (her) and we will say, "This was the LORD's doing, and it is marvelous in our eyes" (Mark 12:11).

Ponder the path of your feet, and let all your ways be established. Do not turn to the right or the left; remove your foot from evil.

PROVERBS 4:26-27

PRAYER NOTES

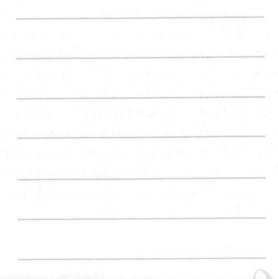

37

If Hardness of Heart Causes Love to Die

LORD, I pray that You would protect my marriage from any hard-heartedness that could develop between us. I pray our hearts will never grow hard toward one another. Take away any pride or bitterness in us so that we will not displease You. I ask that rivers of Your living water will flow in and through us at all times to soften, mend, and restore our hearts (John 7:37-38). Heal any brokenness so that the damage is not irreparable, and take away any scars that form. I ask that we will always feel love for one another in our hearts. Where our hearts have become hard, soften them toward one another.

Keep your heart with all diligence,
for out of it spring the issues of life.

PROVERBS 4:23

PRAYER NOTES

38

If Hardness of Heart Causes Love to Die

———

LORD, You know what is in my heart (Psalm 44:21). Take away all negative thoughts and feelings, and overflow my heart with good things (Psalm 45:1). May the good thoughts in my heart cause my mouth to speak wisdom and not harshness (Psalm 49:3). Create in me a clean heart, and make my spirit right before You (Psalm 51:10). I want to bring to You the sacrifice of a broken spirit and a humble heart (Psalm 51:17). I pray that You would give me a pure heart toward You so that I may stand in Your holy place. Give me clean hands so that I may rise above my situation. Take my heart of stone and give me a heart of love and compassion.

*I will give you a new heart and put a new
spirit within you; I will take the heart of stone out of
your flesh and give you a heart of flesh.*

EZEKIEL 36:26

PRAYER NOTES

_____

_____

_____

_____

_____

_____

39

If Hardness of Heart Causes Love to Die

LORD, restore love in my heart for my husband (wife) if ever I don't feel it anymore. With my whole heart I seek You, and I ask that You would help me hide Your Word in my heart and keep all of Your commandments (Psalm 119:11). Enable me to trust You with all my heart and not depend on my own limited understanding of things. I believe that I will see Your goodness in my life and therefore I will not lose heart. I will wait on You, Lord, and I will stand strong in all I understand of You, knowing that you will strengthen my heart (Psalm 27:13-14). Thank You that You are a God of new beginnings.

*Wait on the LORD; be of good courage,
and He shall strengthen your heart;
wait, I say, on the LORD!*

PSALM 27:14

PRAYER NOTES

40

If Hardness of Heart Causes Love to Die

LORD, I pray that You would give my husband (wife) a heart to know You better so that his (her) heart will be soft toward both You and me. Where his (her) heart has already become hard, I pray that he (she) will turn to You with all of his (her) heart and find Your presence waiting for him (her) (Jeremiah 29:13). Open his (her) heart to hear what You are speaking to him (her) (Acts 16:14). Please help him (her) to have a heart filled with truth and not one that is open to the lies of the enemy. Keep him (her) from having a rebellious spirit and a stubborn heart, and make his (her) heart right before You (Psalm 81:12).

A good man out of the good treasure
of his heart brings forth good things.

MATTHEW 12:3

PRAYER NOTES

_____

_____

_____

_____

_____

_____

41

If You Are No Longer Each Other's Top Priority

LORD, I pray You would help my husband (wife) and me to always make You our top priority, and to make each other our priority under You. Enable us to live in Your love so that we can learn to love each other the way You want us to. Show us how to establish right priorities in our marriage and in our family. I pray that we will not do anything "through selfish ambition or conceit, but in lowliness of mind" may we esteem each other better than ourselves (Philippians 2:3). Help us to always find time for one another to be a help, support, encourager, uplifter, lover, companion, and sharer of good things.

*Cause me to hear Your lovingkindness
in the morning, for in You do I trust;
cause me to know the way in which I should
walk, for I lift up my soul to You.*

PSALM 143:8

PRAYER NOTES

42

If You Are No Longer Each Other's Top Priority

―――

LORD, enable us to always bear the burden of the other concerning the difficult things that happen in life. Help us to choose each other over the other seemingly important things that vie for our attention. Teach us to set aside time to be together alone and to reaffirm each other as our top priority under You. In our seasons of necessary busyness, help us to be understanding of one another and in agreement as to how to handle those times successfully. Thank You that You have chosen us to be people for Yourself, "a special treasure" for Your glory (Deuteronomy 7:6). Help us to always find our treasure in You above all else.

As for me and my house,
we will serve the LORD.

JOSHUA 24:15

PRAYER NOTES

43

If You Are No Longer Each Other's Top Priority

LORD, I look to You to teach me the way I should walk and what I should do (Psalm 143:8). Reveal to me any place where my priorities are off. Show me where I have put other things, people, or activities before You or my husband (wife). If I have made my husband (wife) feel as though he (she) is less than a top priority in my life, help me to apologize to him (her) and make amends for it. Restore us to the place where we should be. Help me to put our children in highest priority, just under You, Lord, and my husband (wife), for I know that the greatest blessing for them is that we stay together.

*Seek first the kingdom of God and
His righteousness, and all these things
shall be added to you.*

MATTHEW 6:33

PRAYER NOTES

44

If You Are No Longer Each Other's Top Priority

LORD, where my husband's (wife's) priorities are out of order, I pray You would help him (her) to realize he (she) needs to put You first, me second, and our children next before everything else. Help him (her) to see where he (she) must make necessary changes in the way he (she) spends time. Bless his (her) work so that he (she) can accomplish more in less time. Enable him (her) to say no to the things which do not please You and are not to be high on the priority list. Help him (her) to clearly see what is most important in life and what is not. Help him (her) to choose the path of humility and righteousness.

Humble yourselves under the mighty hand of God, that He may exalt you in due time, casting all your care upon Him, for He cares for you.

1 Peter 5:6-7

PRAYER NOTES

_____

_____

_____

_____

_____

_____

_____

45

If the "D" Word Becomes an Option

LORD, I pray You would help my husband (wife) and me to rise far above any thoughts of divorce as a solution to our problems or a way out of our marriage. Keep our hearts so close to You and each other that we never even speak the word "divorce" in regard to each other and never harbor the idea of divorce in our minds or hearts. God, help us to always be affectionate to one another, "in honor giving preference to one another" (Romans 12:10). Show us where we are doing things that are breaking our marriage down instead of building it up. Help us to grow stronger in You and learn to treat each other in a way that pleases You.

*Therefore, what God has joined
together, let not man separate.*

Matthew 19:6

Prayer Notes

46

If the "D" Word Becomes an Option

LORD, help us to stand strong together through every problem and to not be afraid to seek outside help when we need it. I repent of any time I have even thought about what it would be like to be married to someone else. I repent of these thoughts before You. I turn to You to find solutions to any problems in my marriage. Whenever I have thought of divorce as an option or a way out of our problems, I ask You to forgive me, for I know it displeases You. I know You hate divorce and it grieves Your Spirit, so I pray that You would help me to never do that again from this day forward.

If two lie down together, they will keep warm;
but how can one be warm alone?

ECCLESIASTES 4:11

PRAYER NOTES

_____

_____

_____

_____

_____

_____

47

If the "D" Word Becomes an Option

LORD, I confess any time that I have ever considered divorce in my mind or have uttered that word to my husband (wife), friends, or family members in regard to my marriage. I reject any spirit of divorce that I have invited into my heart and our marriage by the careless words I have spoken or thoughts I have had. I repent of any time I have even thought about what it would be like to be married to someone else. I recognize these thoughts as evil and adulterous, and I repent of them before You. I turn to You to find solutions to any problems in my marriage. Give me wisdom to do things Your way.

If any brother has a wife who does not believe,
and she is willing to live with him,
let him not divorce her. And a woman who
has a husband who does not believe, if he is willing
to live with her, let her not divorce him.

1 Corinthians 7:12-13

Prayer Notes

_____

_____

_____

_____

_____

_____

48

If the "D" Word Becomes an Option

LORD, where my husband (wife) has entertained thoughts of divorce, I ask that You would open his (her) eyes to see how far away that is from Your best for his (her) life and our lives together. For any time we have discussed divorce or he (she) has used the word "divorce" as a way out of our problems, I come before You on my husband's (wife's) behalf and ask for Your forgiveness. I ask that You would destroy the lie of the enemy that says divorce is an option we should consider. Show him (her) a better way, which is Your way for our lives. Let there be no divorce in our future.

A man shall leave his father and mother and be joined to his wife, and the two shall become one flesh.

EPHESIANS 5:31

PRAYER NOTES

49

If Infidelity Shakes Your Foundation

LORD, I pray You would protect my marriage from any kind of infidelity. May adultery be far from us and never find a place in either of our minds or hearts. Pour Your wisdom and knowledge into us so that we are too wise and too smart to allow the enemy to sneak up on our blind side and throw temptation in our path. I pray You would not allow temptation to even come near us. Keep us far from anyone who would try to lead us into anything evil. Remove anyone from our lives who would ever tempt us with adulterous thoughts. Give us the ability to see danger in advance and the wisdom to not do anything stupid.

Watch and pray, lest you enter into temptation.
The spirit indeed is willing, but the flesh is weak.

MATTHEW 26:41

PRAYER NOTES

_____

_____

_____

_____

_____

_____

_____

_____

50

If Infidelity Shakes Your Foundation

LORD, help me to love You with all my heart, soul, mind, and strength, and help me to love my husband (wife) the same way (Mark 12:30). Keep me far from the broad way that leads to destruction, and help me to always choose the narrow gate that leads to life (Matthew 7:13-14). Thank You for my husband (wife) and for the marriage You have given us. I smash down any dream I have entertained of being loved by someone else. Help me to see this as a false god I have set up to worship in place of You. Help us to live in integrity before You and each other so that we will walk securely (Proverbs 10:9).

No temptation has overtaken you except such as is common to man; but God is faithful, who will not allow you to be tempted beyond what you are able, but with the temptation will also make the way of escape, that you may be able to bear it.

1 CORINTHIANS 10:13

PRAYER NOTES

51

If Infidelity Shakes Your Foundation

LORD, show me anything in me that has given place to infidelity in my heart. Wherever I have thought of another man (woman) and how it would be to be married to him (her) instead of my husband (wife), I confess that as sin. Where I have found myself attracted to someone of the opposite sex who is not my spouse, I also confess that before You as sin. Take all sinful and lustful thoughts out of my heart. I refuse to listen to the lies of the enemy telling me that anything would be better for me than what I have in my husband (wife). Lord, I ask that my desire would always be only for my husband (wife) and no one else.

This is the will of God, your sanctification:
that you should abstain from sexual immorality;
that each of you should know how to possess his
own vessel in sanctification and honor.

1 Thessalonians 4:3-4

PRAYER NOTES

52

If Infidelity Shakes Your Foundation

LORD, I pray You would fill my husband's (wife's) heart with Your Spirit so that it does not wander from me and our marriage to anyone else. Remove from him (her) all opportunities for anything inappropriate or anything that crosses the line of decency. Take away all lust and attraction from his (her) heart and replace it with Your love. Show me all I can do to build him (her) up and be the wife (husband) he (she) needs me to be. Help him (her) to flee all adulterous thoughts and be able to glorify You in his (her) body, soul, and spirit (1 Corinthians 6:18-20). Thank You, Jesus, that You are able to help us when we are tempted.

*In that He Himself has suffered, being tempted,
He is able to aid those who are tempted.*

HEBREWS 2:18

PRAYER NOTES

_____

_____

_____

_____

_____

_____

_____

53

If One of You Decides
to Leave Home

LORD, one of the greatest calamities our marriage could experience would be to separate from one another. I pray that it would never happen to us in any way. Help us to always pray and be watchful about this. Help us to always be in close contact and emotionally current with one another. Open our eyes whenever either of us is blind to what is going on inside the other. Show us where we have been preoccupied with other things and other people. Give us revelation so that we can see the truth and stay on the path You have for us (Proverbs 29:18). If You are *for* us, who can be *against* us? (Romans 8:31).

He Himself has said,
"I will never leave you nor forsake you."
So we may boldly say: "The LORD is my helper;
I will not fear. What can man do to me?"

HEBREWS 13:5-6

PRAYER NOTES

_____

_____

_____

_____

_____

_____

_____

If One of You Decides to Leave Home

———◦———

LORD, I confess any place where I have separated myself in my heart from my husband (wife). I break that hardness in me that has kept me distanced—whether as a self-protective measure or just by being preoccupied with other things. I know any kind of distance between two people, especially whom You have made to be one, goes against Your will. I recognize this state of mind as an offense against You. Thank You that because of Your love for me, I am more than a conqueror, and I can conquer this. Thank You that nothing can ever separate me from Your love (Romans 8:37-39). I will not let my heart be troubled, but I will trust in You instead (John 14:1).

*Count it all joy when you fall into various trials,
knowing that the testing of your faith produces
patience. But let patience have its perfect work, that
you may be perfect and complete, lacking nothing.*

JAMES 1:3-4

PRAYER NOTES

_____

_____

_____

_____

_____

_____

55

If One of You Decides to Leave Home

LORD, I refuse to let myself become anxious about any sense of distance I feel between my husband (wife) and me. Instead, I come to You with thanksgiving for who You are and all that You have done for us, and I let my requests be made known to You. I pray You would protect my marriage from a separation of our hearts. Thank You that Your peace which passes all understanding will keep my heart and mind in Christ Jesus (Philippians 4:6-7). I know that Your grace is sufficient for me and Your strength is made perfect in my weakness. I can trust that when I am weak You will make me strong, because I depend on You (2 Corinthians 12:9-10).

*Two are better than one, because they
have a good reward for their labor. For if they fall,
one will lift up his companion.*

ECCLESIASTES 4:9-10

PRAYER NOTES

_____

_____

_____

_____

_____

_____

56

If One of You Decides to Leave Home

LORD, where my husband (wife) has separated from me in any way—whether physically, emotionally, or mentally—I pray You would bring him (her) back. Thank You, Lord, that even though he (she) may leave me, You have promised that You never will (Deuteronomy 31:6). Lord, I pray for restoration of any emotional and physical separation between us. Change our hearts and help me to be everything he (she) needs me to be. Restore us emotionally together again. Give me courage and strength to fight for our relationship until it is the way You want it to be. You are a good God, and we will find the greatest blessings by following You and trusting in Your ways (Psalm 34:8).

The LORD will perfect that which concerns me;
Your mercy, O Lord, endures forever;
do not forsake the works of Your hands.

PSALM 138:8

PRAYER NOTES

_____

_____

_____

_____

_____

_____

57

If Hope Seems Lost and You Need a Miracle

LORD, I pray You would help my husband (wife) and me to never fall into hopelessness, especially with regard to our relationship and marriage. Help us to grow strong in faith—faith in You and in each other. Help us to put our hope in You, for You are our helper and protector (Psalm 33:20). May Your unfailing love and favor rest on us (Psalm 33:22). Enable us to inherit all You have for us because we have hope in our hearts (Psalm 37:9). May our marriage become all You want it to be. Even in times where we may suffer hurt or misunderstanding, I believe You are able to keep all we have committed to You (2 Timothy 1:12).

For everyone who asks receives, and he who seeks finds, and to him who knocks it will be opened.

MATTHEW 7:8

PRAYER NOTES

_____

_____

_____

_____

_____

_____

58

If Hope Seems Lost and You Need a Miracle

LORD, I pray we will always have patience to wait for You to work in our lives and our marriage. Thank You that because You were crucified and resurrected from the dead, we can have hope that You will resurrect anything in our lives no matter how dead and hopeless it may seem (1 Peter 1:3). Help us to "let patience have its perfect work" in us so that we "may be perfect and complete, lacking nothing" (James 1:4). Help us to keep our eyes on You. I pray that You would help us to not hesitate to hope again out of fear that we will be disappointed. Lord, we commit to trusting in You at all times.

O Israel, put your hope in the LORD,
for with the LORD is unfailing love and with
him is full redemption.

PSALM 130:7 NIV

PRAYER NOTES

_____

_____

_____

_____

_____

_____

_____

59

If Hope Seems Lost and You Need a Miracle

———

LORD, I commit my husband (wife) into Your hands. I pray that any hopelessness he (she) has felt about himself (herself) will be taken out of his (her) heart. Make him (her) all You created him (her) to be. Break down any strongholds in his (her) mind where hopelessness has been allowed to reign. Help him (her) to put his (her) hope in You and understand that it is not by our might or power, but by Your Spirit that our relationship can be transformed to become all it was made to be. Take away any hopelessness he (she) feels about me, our marriage, and our life together. Thank You that You are the God of hope (Romans 15:13).

*Those who wait on the LORD shall
renew their strength; they shall mount up with
wings like eagles, they shall run and not be weary,
they shall walk and not faint.*

ISAIAH 40:31

PRAYER NOTES

_____

_____

_____

_____

_____

_____

60

If Hope Seems Lost and You Need a Miracle

LORD, help my husband (wife) to understand that because of You our situation is never hopeless (John 14:26). Even though we may have difficulties, we are not crushed because You sustain us. We don't have to live with despair because our hope is in You. "We are hard pressed on every side, yet not crushed; we are perplexed, but not in despair" (2 Corinthians 4:8). I pray that the eyes of his (her) understanding will be opened so that he (she) may know the hope of Your calling on his (her) life, and come to understand "what is the exceeding greatness" of Your power toward those who believe (Ephesians 1:18-19). I will be strong and take heart because my hope is in You (Psalm 31:24).

*The righteous cry out, and the LORD hears,
and delivers them out of all their troubles.*

PSALM 34:17 NIV

PRAYER NOTES

_____

_____

_____

_____

_____

_____

Other Books
by Stormie Omartian

The Power of Prayer™ to Change Your Marriage
Stormie Omartian encourages husbands or wives to pray to protect their relationship from 14 serious threats that can lead to unsatisfying marriages or even divorce. Biblical, prayerful insights addressing communication breakdown, struggles with finances, anger, infidelity, parenting struggles, and more, will lead couples to healing and restoration.

The Power of a Praying® Wife
Stormie shares how wives can develop a deeper relationship with their husbands by praying for them. With this practical advice on praying for specific areas, including decision making, fears, spiritual strength, and sexuality, women will discover the fulfilling marriage God intended.

The Power of a Praying® Husband
Building on the success of *The Power of a Praying® Wife*, Stormie offers this guide to help husbands pray more effectively for their wives. Each chapter features comments from well-known Christian men, biblical wisdom, and prayer ideas.

The Power of a Praying® Parent
This powerful book for parents offers 30 easy-to-read chapters that focus on specific areas of prayers for children. This personal, practical guide leads the way to enriched, strong prayer lives for both moms and dads.

Just Enough Light for the Step I'm On
New Christians and those experiencing life changes or difficult times will appreciate Stormie's honesty, candor, and advice based on experience and the Word of God in this collection of devotional readings perfect for the pressures of today's world.